AN INSIDER'S GUIDE TO
INTERIOR DESIGN FOR
SMALL SPACES

How to Create a Beautiful Home Quickly, Effectively and on a Budget

EXPERT DESIGN AND DECORATING TIPS

GAIL GREEN

D1546064

For information about this title or to order other books and/or electronic media, contact the publisher:

Zero Circle Publishing
7014 13th Avenue, Suite 202
Brooklyn, NY 11228

ISBN: 978-0-9862875-1-0
       978-0-9862875-0-3 (Print)

Printed in the United States of America

Table of Contents

- **Legal Disclaimer**   v

- **A Note From the Author**   1

- **Who Should Read This Guide**   2

- **What Information Is Covered**   2

- **Key Concepts**   5

- **Designing Your Space!**   10

     DO-IT-YOURSELF (WITHOUT A DESIGNER)   11

         Color and Paint   12

         Furniture Selection and Arrangement   26

         Lighting   49

     WITH A DESIGNER   55

         Color and Paint   61

         Furniture Selection and Arrangement   73

         Lighting   80

     SMALL RENOVATIONS   81

         Lighting   84

         Architectural Changes   90

- **Additional Tricks of the Trade!**   **106**

    Do-It-Yourself (Without a Designer)   106

    With a Designer   112

    Small Renovations   115

- **Trade Descriptions**   **119**

- **About the Author**   **123**

- **About the Architects**   **123**

- **Acknowledgements**   **124**

- **Sources**   **125**

- **Bonus**   **128**

A Note From the Author

Interior design is about much more than merely having good taste. Designing elegant and chic interiors requires knowledge, resourcefulness and creativity, especially in small spaces.

As with most art forms, interior design is highly subjective; however, with the right focus and planning, it can be an exciting and cost-effective adventure with instant returns and extraordinary, long-lasting results — in other words, a profitable investment.

When it comes to small spaces, however, there is a common misconception that it is not worth the time or money that it takes to create a beautiful home. Conversely, many overspend and overdecorate their spaces because they do not have proper direction.

The intention of this guide is to not only present you with valuable options but also to describe those options to you to the extent that you can make an educated decision as to whether to pursue the changes — on your own or with the help of a professional. Specifically, you will learn professional tricks and techniques for transforming small spaces into beautiful, upscale dwellings while saving significant time, money and energy. The strategies that will be discussed have been successfully implemented for more than 30 years and reflect inventive problem solving.

After reading through this material, that knowledge will be yours to use as you wish!

Who Should Read This Guide

This book is for anyone interested in learning simple, effective and practical home-design solutions for any type of space; however, it is particularly valuable for small spaces — such as studio or one-bedroom apartments, or even small rooms — which are common in urban settings.

Although the ideas here do not pertain solely to any one type of living space, the term *apartment* has been used throughout for simplicity. The information presented can also benefit those looking to spruce up starter homes, guest homes, smaller second homes or investment homes.

What Information Is Covered

This guide is divided into distinct focus areas that have been carefully selected in response to a common question: ***Where and how should I focus my interior design efforts to achieve the*** *most noticeable results in the least amount of time?* These key areas — if you're interested in a basic framework for a remarkable outcome within a reasonable time frame — are as follows: color and paint, furniture arrangement and selection, lighting and architectural changes. Architectural ideas and viewpoints communicated here are largely based on or supported by projects and philosophies of one of New York City's leading architectural firms, David Estreich Architects.

The sections have been further organized into the following three categories where applicable:

Do-It-Yourself (Without a Designer): A do-it-yourself (DIY) approach that does not involve construction or architectural changes. All enhancements are strictly decorative and can be performed without the expertise of a professional.

Pros	Cons
• Minimal cost	• Final outcome is uncertain
• Sense of control	• Higher probability of error
• Quick results	• Potential for costing more (both in time and money)

With a Designer: When the desired changes are pursued with the expertise and experience of a professional. Here, the primary focus is on soft furnishings (furniture and accessories) without construction or the use of a contractor.

Pros	Cons
• More likely to achieve or exceed expectations • Cost savings on better-quality materials • Longer-lasting and more impressive results • Unique and custom solutions • More efficient use of time • Transfer of knowledge and information	• Additional time and effort to identify, select and work with a designer • Potential for differences in vision • Expectations may not be met • Possible cost overages

Small Renovations: Using a professional with specialized construction knowledge (meaning an architect or advanced designer) and a contractor to implement architectural changes or enhancements to a space.

Pros	Cons
• Can increase the value and purchase price of the home • Better functioning and more flexible space • Customized results • Permanent and longer-lasting results • More unique and makes a big impression	• Higher initial costs • Takes longer • Inconvenience of renovating while living in the space • Coordinating and planning with multiple parties • May require pre-approval by the building • Fear of the unknown (e.g., where to start, total cost, timing, end results)

Key Concepts

Many of the reoccurring concepts cited throughout this guide relate to the following four interconnected design theories, which contribute significantly to the end result of the suggested tips. If applied properly, these strategies provide valuable benefits, such as enhanced space, comfort, harmony, interest, function and aesthetic appeal.

#1. CONSISTENCY

It is overwhelming and distracting when too much is going on in a studio or one-bedroom apartment. The effect is similar to that of a pinball machine — how your eye bounces around from object to object without a stable resting place. That's why it is important to establish consistency in your space. This effect can be achieved throughout an apartment by decorating with the same (or similar) colors, fabrics, proportions, textures and furniture styles.

Simply put: Less is more. Less color variation used more effectively, for instance, creates a more powerful statement. This is especially true in a small space, as individual objects tend to stand out more than they would in a larger environment. When you have less to work with, how you use what you have becomes more significant. Creating relationships between the items in your apartment as well as with the architecture is an effective method for optimizing and personalizing your space.

Consistency is what will help communicate a strong message within your home. Building a consistently designed space with a sense of visual flow is an essential component for instilling your home with meaning.

Deeper Understanding

Think about some of the best novels and films — they all find creative and ingenious ways of connecting the elements within a story to support an underlying theme deemed to be meaningful. Likewise, it is equally important (if not more so) to do the same with your home.

#2. DEFINITION OF SPACE

In simple terms, definition of space means allocating different interior areas for primary functions: eating, bathing, resting, entertaining. A few examples of common areas that people usually define immediately are the dining room, living room, kitchen, sleeping area and bathroom. By defining your space, you create a personal map within your home.

As you will see throughout this guide, there are many ways that you can define your space, including maintaining a sense of consistency, relating furniture through alignment and accentuating particular elements through "framing." Another way to define a space is to introduce particular elements that have a clear meaning or purpose, such as televisions (entertainment), place mats (eating) or desks (work).

Defining your space plays an important role in creating an ambience that will make you feel relaxed and comfortable.

Deeper Understanding

Imagine you are strapped for time and under pressure to get something done. You need quick, specific and comprehensive answers immediately, so you call up a friend. Now, think about how annoying it would be if that friend were to explain things to you in a broad, general and undefined way. You'd be pretty frustrated because you wouldn't be able to interpret what that person was saying. As a result, you wouldn't get what you need, which would cause feelings of confusion and restlessness.

#3. PROPORTION AND BALANCE

You can attain a sense of solace every day by having a home that is proportional and balanced. A personal setting that fosters stability and security is an important outlet for counterbalancing the distractions or stress that may come from everyday life.

You have the ability to influence how you feel when you're at home. With this in mind, you should create a space that is a reflection of how you *want* to feel. From an interior design perspective, words such as *proportion, balance, scale, symmetry* and *harmony* are all essentially alluding to the same thing: a feeling of order and comfort within your space. There is an inherent value in proportion and how we relate to our spaces. Proportion not only provides comfort but also is linked with beauty (aesthetics); however, when it comes to designing your home to achieve all these valuable benefits, it may be difficult to figure out where to start.

You will see that many of the tips mentioned in this guide have an element specifically designed for achieving balance and proportion.

Deeper Understanding

Without thinking twice, people easily spend thousands of dollars a year on yoga classes and related initiatives to balance the mind and the body. Why? Because it feels good. A healthy mind is a healthy spirit. The same concept applies to your home.

#4. FOCAL POINTS AND DESTINATION POINTS

Focal points are visual destinations that naturally capture a person's attention. From a design perspective, they are important because they offer the eye a comfortable resting place (and are usually located near eye level). For this reason, focal points can subconsciously provide more relaxing and peaceful atmospheres.

When interior space is limited, it is important to control where you want focal points to be. By keeping patterns and bold colors to a minimum, you are able to direct the eye to specific areas or pieces. Intense patterns and eye-catching colors can produce a potentially unwanted focal point that may divert attention and cause disorientation.

By understanding how to create and manipulate focal points, you can control what parts of your space are accentuated and which parts are best subdued. When selecting a destination point, it is important to consider several things: that the element is relatively more aesthetically pleasing than the other surrounding pieces, that the element fits well with the rest of the room and its components, and that it is centrally located in the room at eye level (if possible) — and looks attractive at that height. It is helpful to think of this exercise as a composition, in which all of the pieces fit together in a complementary way.

Deeper Understanding

If everything has the same level of importance in your space, nothing will feel special. It is quite rare for a person to be completely ambivalent toward all objects in his or her home. People instinctually place more emotion or value on things that they perceive as important. By selectively differentiating areas or items in your space, you'll evoke stronger emotions and interest. A natural tendency is to accentuate favorable focal points and de-emphasize less-appealing features or views.

Designing Your Space!

When designing your home, the goal should be to love how you feel when you walk through your door, each and every time.

DO-IT-YOURSELF (WITHOUT A DESIGNER)

The obvious appeal of the DIY approach is undoubtedly the savings that come from doing all the work and buying everything yourself. The more subtle appeal is the sense of control that the DIYer has over the outcome. Many DIYers get a thrill out of successfully accomplishing a project on their own without professional assistance. For those looking for quick and effective results at little or no cost, this may be the way to go.

The downside is that the final outcome is uncertain. The DIY project could end up costing twice as much money as originally estimated — and take up twice as much time — if the wrong materials are purchased, if the plan backfires or if the DIYer is ultimately not happy with the finished product.

If you choose the DIY route, the following tips and techniques offer many creative ideas for how to improve your space.

The price information provided herein is for reference purposes only and is based on New York City estimates. Although the author has made every attempt to provide price information that is representative, the prices noted below are intended to reflect the author's viewpoint on what is an expected or reasonable cost for which the relevant tip or technique may be addressed while also keeping true to the specific objectives and high-quality standards expressed in this guide. The actual price will depend on a variety of factors, including the quality of service/materials, location, the current market and the scope of work. Further, there may be additional cost-saving opportunities associated with bundling activities as part of a project rather than making a series of one-off purchases, as larger projects tend to offer the benefit of economies of scale and additional deals and negotiations.

COLOR AND PAINT

A new paint job is one of the best ways to get the most bang for your buck: It can be fast, easy and inexpensive and achieve big results. Nevertheless, people tend to skip this step because they think their current paint job is in decent shape. But here's something most people either don't know or don't pay attention to: When you move into a new rental or purchased apartment, the objective of the paint job you inherit is usually to simply hide imperfections and cover the surface area — not to enhance the space's aesthetic appeal. This is because landlords, superintendents and building managers can save money by doing several quick paint jobs at once. As a result, they often use paint that's cheaper (meaning of poorer quality), darker pigmented (to better camouflage imperfections) and diluted with water or paint thinner (to create more paint, thus gaining extra coverage). Do you really want to live with a paint job that's aligned to those efforts? To instantly transform your space, Select The Right Paint Color, Apply The Correct Paint Finish and Choose A High-Quality Paint Brand.

SELECT THE RIGHT PAINT COLOR

Paint allows you to control and influence the mood and style of your apartment. But before setting out to the nearest paint store to clear the shelves, you should know the kind of atmosphere you want your apartment to reflect and understand that the ambience will be affected by the colors that you choose. An often overlooked consideration is that colors change based on all kinds of factors: room size and shape; what direction your apartment faces (north, south, east or west); even time of day. Those factors will also influence how a small paint sample in a fluorescently lit store will look when applied to a wall at home. For example, a wall may appear periwinkle blue in the sun but resemble lavender in the shade. Meanwhile, color tends to expand and deepen when it is applied to a wall surface. For instance, a green that has black tints is likely to absorb light and appear darker, whereas a lime green with white traces is likely to evoke the opposite effect and become brighter.

In order to properly evaluate a color (this goes for white, too), request a large sample or small pint of the color you are considering. Take it home, apply it to your wall and observe how its appearance changes over several days. It is also important to determine how it looks in relation to the other paint colors in the room, as well as with your existing furniture and fabrics.

At a basic level, without getting into too many technicalities, here are some essential things to know about color:

- *Darker colors.* In general, black and colors with hints of black are viewed as darker colors. Dark colors tend to absorb light and thus are less reflective, resulting in a space that looks darker.

- *Warmer colors.* In general, orange, red and yellow, and colors with hints of these hues, are viewed as warm colors. Warm colors tend to make you think of sunlight and heat.

In order to simplify the complicated concept of color, it helps to think about darker and warmer colors together. Darker colors can have varying levels of warmth, and warmer colors can have varying levels of darkness. The important thing to know is that when used on walls, darker and warmer colors make the surface look as though it is advancing (or coming toward you). The result is a space that feels cozier and more intimate.

As with darker and warmer colors, it helps to think about lighter and cooler colors together.

- *Lighter colors.* In general, white and colors with hints of white are viewed as lighter colors. Lighter colors tend to reflect light, resulting in a space that looks brighter.

- *Cooler colors.* In general, blue, green and light purple, and colors with hints of these hues, are viewed as cool colors. Cool colors tend to make you think of sky and water.

When used on walls, lighter and cooler colors make the surface look as though it is receding (or moving away from you). The result is a space that feels bigger and calmer.

The best way to determine the degree to which a color absorbs or reflects light is to refer to its Light Reflectance Value (LRV), which is usually indicated on the manufacturer's packaging (such as the paint can or paint chip). Simply put, the LRV is a measurement that uses a 0 to 100 percent scale, with 0 percent representing absolute black and 100 percent reflecting absolute white. The Land of Color's website does an excellent job of breaking this down.

See Color and Paint for additional details regarding color, including its influence on space. If you want a deeper understanding of color and how to apply it correctly, you should consult with a professional. Interior designers are trained to interpret LRV and determine the right color based on attributes like color temperature.

If You Are Going to Use One Paint Color, Go With a Pure and Highly Reflective White

When deciding what color to paint your apartment, don't overlook white. It's a simple but powerful color: It can make a small space appear brighter, lighter, sharper and more spacious and airy. While lighter colors in general have this impact, it's particularly true for pure, non-tinted and highly reflective whites.

Although you might not realize it, the white ceiling paint used for a default paint job is often a non-pure grayish white, and the default wall paint is often a lighter and brighter white but still non-pure. This means that your ceiling is actually a slightly different color from your walls — an important point as this can disrupt continuity. Painting the ceiling and walls the same pure white will open up your space and smooth visual and physical boundaries.

One important thing to note is that white inherently reflects light independent of the finish (more on Apply The Correct Paint Finish later). So if you use a pure white that is highly reflective, you will fully leverage your ability to make the best use of light within your apartment. Any paint store will be able to direct you to a highly reflective white.

Add Pops of Your Favorite Color to Unusual Places

Many people have a favorite color that they would love to use for their apartment, but, for one reason or another, it just doesn't work — maybe it throws off the theme of the apartment, or it doesn't look good on a large scale. But you don't have to rule out the color altogether.

One fun technique is to use a splash of your favorite color in an unexpected place. This method works best in settings where the furniture and walls are neutral, meaning colors such as white, black, gray, beige or ivory. (In general, neutral colors quiet a space by making it more recessive and less chaotic.) A pop of color may seem like a small change — and it is — but it packs a strong punch: It accentuates the color, creates an intriguing focal point and personalizes your space.

If you have a color you'd like to play around with, identify a surprising place within the room where not too much is going on visually. Select or purchase an object with this color and place the object in the chosen location for a couple of days. If you are happy with how it looks, consider painting that area, or a nearby area, the same color.

This technique doesn't have to be limited to paint. A colorful piece of furniture or accessory, such as a throw pillow, can do the trick, too.

Here are some suggestions for easy places within your apartment to experiment with pops of color:

- *Kitchen.* The best place to visually enhance the kitchen is the backsplash, which is the panel behind the sink or stove that protects the wall from splashes. This option is especially applicable if no tile is in this area. By investing in an interesting backsplash with some color variation, the whole space benefits from a simple enrichment since the backsplash is where the eye most comfortably settles.

- *Bedroom.* If your bedroom is painted a neutral color and you would like to add a quick dash of color without doing anything too permanent, buy a colorful bedspread and pillows to create a temporary splash.

- *Living room.* For a conservative approach, add color by applying a colorful trim or welting to a sofa or by cleverly placing artwork or smaller colorful items, such as a vase with flowers.

Be Strategic When Using Multiple Paint Colors for the Walls

As mentioned earlier, the concept of "less is more" is especially important for smaller spaces. When it comes to color, less used more effectively creates a larger impact. Too many colors used throughout an apartment introduce unwanted noise and distraction.

If you are looking to apply more than one paint color (counting white as a color), it's generally best to use one primary color (the *dominant* color, preferably white or a lighter color) and one different color (the *contrast* color). The dominant color should be used more liberally and the contrast color more sparingly. This strategy will add to the room's appeal without making it too hectic.

To test the waters, try painting two intersecting walls (walls that meet at a right angle) the same contrast color. For example, if you've selected white as your dominant color and light green as your contrast color, you should paint the two intersecting walls the exact same light green and the two other walls and ceiling the exact same white.

A bolder way to add a contrast color is to paint one wall and the ceiling within the room the same contrast color. This option will make the room appear larger because the contrast color wall will flow nicely into the ceiling, visually combining the two spaces and establishing a sense of continuity.

In instances in which you have a recessed wall — meaning two parallel walls on the same plane — it is important that the same color is used for the entire plane. By using the same color, you can establish a visual illusion that adds depth while simultaneously introducing enhanced definition without causing a distraction. Different colors or shades may further accentuate definition if done correctly; however, you should probably consult a professional if you want to go this route, as this technique can backfire and add too much noise. See Create a Recessed Wall for more information on what a recessed wall is and how to paint it.

APPLY THE CORRECT PAINT FINISH

Paint colors are sold in different types of finishes, and the finish type will usually be listed directly on the paint can. A finish is not a paint type but rather the paint's "effect," meaning whether the painted surface will appear smooth, reflective and so forth. Each finish has a variety of different benefits, ranging from better longevity to easier maintenance to better durability to more-attractive surface areas. These days, many companies develop specialty finishes for specific purposes, materials or effects, so when you're at the paint store, it is important to communicate what you will be using the finish for so you can be directed toward the most appropriate product.

In general, finishes are categorized as either flat or glossy, though the degree to which paint is flat or glossy varies greatly. The general spectrum is:

Matte *(the flattest)* ➜ Eggshell ➜ Satin ➜ Semigloss ➜
High Gloss *(the glossiest)*

The extent to which paint is flat or glossy influences two key surface characteristics:

- *Reflectivity.* In regard to finishes, the *less* light reflected by the paint finish (meaning the flatter the paint), the *less* you'll notice surface imperfections (like bumps and wall scars). The *more* light reflected by the paint finish (meaning the glossier the paint), the *more* you'll notice surface imperfections. Keep in mind that the above-discussed LRV measurement for paint color does not take into account any reflectivity that might be attributed to a paint finish.

- *Durability.* The *less* durable the paint finish (meaning the flatter the paint), the *harder* it is to maintain and clean. The *more* durable the paint finish (meaning the glossier the paint), the *easier* the paint is to maintain and clean.

Here's a cheat sheet to help you keep tabs on these varying attributes:

Finish Type	Reflectivity	Durability
Flatter	Reflects less light, so you'll notice *fewer* surface imperfections	Less durable, making it *harder* to maintain and clean
Glossier	Reflects more light, so you'll notice *more* surface imperfections	More durable, making it *easier* to maintain and clean

There are three primary factors to consider when selecting a paint finish:

- The current condition of what you're painting (in terms of surface imperfections)

- The level of exposure to light

- The expected traffic and contact potential

Here are the common finish choices for various areas within your apartment:

- *Ceiling. Flat finish.* Ceilings are out of reach, so durability is less important; however, ceilings are a focal point for light — they naturally attract more light compared with other surfaces — which is why a less reflective finish is preferable.

- *Walls. Eggshell finish.* With walls, durability is a chief consideration given the likelihood of contact. An eggshell finish tends to have just enough gloss to withstand day-to-day wear and tear and just enough flatness to minimize imperfections. However, for walls in the kitchen or bathroom — where you are more likely to connect with surfaces since the spaces are smaller and are used for purposes that require heavy traffic — you should consider using additional gloss, such as that found in a satin finish.

- *Woodwork (doors, baseboards, moldings). Satin finish.* These areas of the apartment tend to protrude or get knocked up, so use a satin finish for protection. For baseboards and other areas that are closer to the floor and less visible, a semigloss finish might be more appropriate to guard against additional contact from vacuum cleaners and chair legs.

It is worth noting that the interior design market is constantly changing, so it is important to always discuss your objectives with a knowledgeable paint-store employee, as there may be additional products that you can use in conjunction with the correct finish to enhance the look that you are going for.

To get a sense of how much you will be able to enhance the appeal of your apartment with a new paint job, ask your landlord, superintendent or building manager for a list of the specific paints and finishes used for each surface area in your apartment. Assess the current conditions of the ceilings and walls as compared with the information in this section.

Is all this talk of paint finishes making your head spin? A designer might be helpful in this area to assess the current condition and durability of your walls and recommend specific paint finishes.

CHOOSE A HIGH-QUALITY PAINT BRAND

Just as there are many types of paint finishes, there are also many levels of paint quality. Some of the more trusted and quality brands are Benjamin Moore, Farrow & Ball, Sherwin-Williams, Fine Paints of Europe and Pratt & Lambert. (These brands' websites often have helpful color resources, like Benjamin Moore's Color Gallery and Personal Color Viewer.) High-quality paints provide better coverage and longer-lasting results. They are also less likely to splatter during application (and less likely to leave unattractive brush or roller marks); less susceptible to fading and staining; better at hiding wall blemishes; and easier to clean (because they are tougher and smoother, which makes them ideal for scrubbing and washing). In the end, you will save money by buying better-quality paint.

PAINT APPLICATION BASICS

Most paint jobs involve plaster walls, Sheetrock walls or woodwork (doors, baseboards, cabinetry, window sills, moldings).

Regardless of what you're painting, it's important to sand your surface first in order to even out any pre-existing roughness. At a basic level, sanding is a labor-intensive job that involves purchasing sandpaper and a sanding pole (for attaching the paper so that you don't have to sand with your hand). Unfortunately, there are very few services — if any — that offer stand-alone wall sanding, as this activity is usually lumped in if you hire someone to paint. So if you are painting yourself, you will probably have to sand yourself.

After you've sanded, plan on applying two coats of paint. The first coat (the *undercoat*) is a preparatory and protective layer used to cover the pre-existing color and conceal surface imperfections. The second coat (the *finish coat*, not to be confused with the paint finish) should be applied once the undercoat is dry, usually 24 hours later.

Paint jobs involving woodwork usually require an additional primer, which is a protective layer applied *before* the undercoat and finish coat. Wood, which absorbs paint differently than Sheetrock or plaster, requires a glossy paint finish. Because there are many different types of wood, it helps to take a picture of the wood you are painting and present it to a store employee who can provide guidance and suggest supplemental products that might enhance your paint job's results.

You'll usually need to purchase paint rollers for painting larger surfaces (entire walls) and paintbrushes for painting smaller surfaces (chair rails and baseboards) and hard-to-reach areas (corners, crevices). Better-quality rollers and brushes tend to produce smoother strokes and more evenly applied coats of paint, whereas those of poorer quality may be less effective and, say, leave brush hairs on the wall. When at the paint store, be sure to describe what you are painting and request good-quality materials as opposed to trying to save a few bucks. Doing so will make the job easier and produce better results.

Although subject to change, an average or reasonable price range for high-quality paint for a 500-square-foot apartment may be between $150 and $200. The application of primer is an additional cost and may be between $25 and $50. Paint rollers and brushes, depending on quality, may be about $50. The cost for sanding materials (sandpaper and a pole sander) for an apartment in decent shape may be between $25 and $35. If you choose to hire someone to paint for you (excluding all materials), an average or reasonable price range for a qualified professional to paint this space may be between $2,000 and $4,000. You will always be able to find someone willing to paint your space for less; however, if you have high expectations for the results that you will get, you should be confident in the quality of the painting service and its expertise. If you have to repaint the entire space in one or two years, it might not be worth it to save a few bucks up front.

The inherent cost with paint relates to the preparation and existing condition of the walls. If the walls are in good condition and only two coats of paint are required after light sanding, then the costs are lower and less paint is needed. If the walls need repair work, then the exercise becomes costly and more paint is required, especially if the walls need to be skim-coated, which is basically refinishing the wall with fresh plaster. An average or reasonable price range for skim coating an 8-foot-by-12-foot wall (labor plus materials) may be between $1,200 and $3,000, depending on the current state of the wall.

DIY COLOR AND PAINT CHECKLIST
Suggested Steps:

- Determine what kind of look or feel you want your apartment to achieve, and understand that your paint choices will affect the ambience. This includes settling on whether you prefer to use one color consistently throughout or multiple colors.

- Determine what you would like to paint: one wall, one room or the whole apartment.

- Create a list of the finishes you'll need to apply to each surface area. Always review and confirm this list with a knowledgeable employee at the retail store where you will make your purchases.

- Conduct some basic research on what colors will best achieve your desired look or feel.

- Ensure that the wall(s) you choose to paint will fit nicely with the surrounding walls or rooms, and keep consistent with the theme (unless you plan on changing subsequent rooms to fit the new look).

- Determine how the desired colors will appear in your apartment and how the colors will be influenced by light and the time of day. At the paint store, request a paint sample or purchase a small tub of the paint color that you desire and bring it home with you. Remember: Make sure the paint is high quality and that the sample is large enough to provide an accurate representation of the depth and vibrancy of the color(s) chosen.

- Observe the sample in its ultimate location over a few days to see its gradation of hues and determine how you feel.

- Purchase your new paint, and either hire a professional to assist with the paint job or do it yourself. If you hire others to obtain paint for you, request that they provide you with unopened cans of paint prior to beginning the job.

- If you decide to conduct the paint job yourself, apply at least two coats of paint. The first coat is used as a preparatory and protective layer to cover the pre-existing coat color and any holes or imperfections in the surface. The second coat is applied once the first paint coat is dry, usually 24 hours later. Wood requires an extra primer before the first coat of paint.

FURNITURE SELECTION AND ARRANGEMENT

Now that you've mastered what to do with your walls, it's time to move on to furniture and accessories.

SELECT THE RIGHT FURNITURE COLORS

An apartment's furniture-color scheme should, for the most part, be consistent from room to room. Keep in mind that — like what you learned about paint — various factors impact furniture color, such as the amount of light in a room or the color of surrounding objects. A gray sofa may look pure gray in a store but blue at home if you position it next to furniture that accentuates its blue tones. Likewise, because the eye mixes and blends adjacent colors, if you place a gray couch next to a brown wall, the gray will appear dramatically different than if placed against a white or blue wall.

Request fabric swatches and see how the fabric colors respond to your apartment. By paying attention to the amount of light that enters a room, how the time of day influences the level of light and the overall color scheme of the apartment (how the different colors of a room influence each other), you will be positioned to properly pick furniture colors.

USE FURNITURE AND ACCESSORIES THAT HAVE DUAL FUNCTIONALITY

When space is limited, it's smart to use multipurpose furniture — beds, ottomans, benches — that can provide extra functions, such as storage capabilities. By using a piece that has two or three purposes, you can buy less furniture and save more space. For example:

- A set of ottomans can serve as both conversational seating in the living room and extra seating at the dining room table.

- Benches can be used to accommodate conversational seating or dining seating.

- Coffee tables can operate as work surfaces as well as dining tables.

- A desk can be used as a dining table when eating or entertaining.

- A foyer entry table can be used as a dining room table.

- Nesting tables that band together into one small table can expand as necessary into several tables.

- A sculptural bookcase that rises almost all the way to the ceiling can divide a space, serving as both a wall and a storage unit. The bottom of the bookcase can function as enclosed cabinetry, and the top can remain open as shelves.

- A 30- to 36-inch-high cabinet can perform the same fake-wall trick as a bookcase: It can separate spaces — and even hide a TV and stereo system (provided that the back of the unit piece is just as appealing as the front).

For convenience, try using a furniture theme that allows you to tuck away moveable pieces, such as storing ottomans or benches under tables so that you can save space and pull them out when necessary. An added benefit is to find furniture with rollers, such as chairs or desks that have balls on the legs and can be easily moved around the apartment. Ottomans with rolling casters can shift to the living room, dining area or desk for extra seating or to the couch for the legs to rest over.

It can be tempting to go crazy with double-duty furniture. But rather than flood your apartment with multifunctional pieces, take inventory of your space and select items that satisfy your most immediate needs, like storage, seating, table/desk space and shelving.

CHOOSE FURNITURE THAT IS PROPORTIONAL TO YOUR SPACE

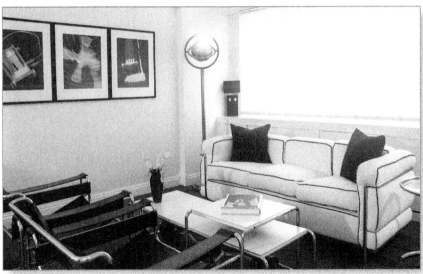

A room needs to be balanced with furniture that is proportionally sized to fit the space. In a small room, large and bulky upholstered furniture will visually shrink the interior. Instead, when designing small spaces, select pieces that look airy. This will de-emphasize the furniture and make the space appear larger and more open. You can also soften the room by using rounded pieces as opposed to those that are more angular. Additionally, smaller-scale furniture, such as a sofa that is 7 feet long instead of 8 feet, will fit the space better and allow for more room around the piece.

One trick is to use furniture with visible legs that add a weightless appearance. Pieces without arms, such as armless sofas and slipper chairs (a chair with a low seat, high back and no arms), exude airiness. One application of this could be using only armless side chairs in the dining room, as side chairs are less cumbersome than armchairs. To make the dining table and chairs appear as if they are taking up less space, place an equal set of side chairs on either side of the table and no chairs at the ends. This type of arrangement will expose the table base and provide the table with a more open appearance.

Another way to achieve an airy effect: Skip heavy-looking wooden, upholstered or leather pieces, and instead use metal (chrome, black metal or stainless steel) furniture that is tubular (pieces with legs and arms that appear thin, round and hollow, like a tube). In addition to allowing the space to breathe, metal furniture is also physically lighter and easier to move, which is helpful for a number of reasons, including entertaining guests, cleaning and otherwise changing up the space. If you don't like the tubular look, try furniture with recessed bases (furniture where the foundation, or the part that holds the furniture up, is discreet and appears hidden). Recessed bases give off a floating feel, too.

Glass is another material that is highly effective in small spaces. Glass tabletops (or other transparent, weightless-looking pieces made of glass or Lucite) create the perception of more floor space.

One small step you can play with: Identify the largest and heaviest piece of furniture in your apartment (table, bed, desk) and start by replacing that object with something lighter and more open, as described above.

PAY ATTENTION TO FURNITURE ARRANGEMENT

Most people unconsciously (or consciously) align longer pieces of furniture parallel to the room's longer direction. Other common decorating tendencies include scattering random pieces of furniture throughout the apartment, pushing furniture as close as possible toward the walls and inadvertently using awkwardly placed windows or doors as focal points. By avoiding these inclinations and adhering to the following techniques, you can achieve better circulation throughout the room, maintain better balance and make a stronger decorating statement.

Align Furniture Based on the Shape of the Room

Studio and one-bedroom apartments are usually disproportion-ate in size, having more of a rectangular railroad feel. Aligning longer pieces of furniture — sofas/couches, beds, tables, desks — parallel to the longer direction of the room exaggerates already emphasized dimensions, which is not ideal. The "tunnel" feel is something to avoid.

The better approach is to do the exact opposite, and place your sofa or long tables along the shorter walls. For instance, if a room is 12 feet by 20 feet, the emphasis is naturally on the longer 20-foot wall, not the shorter 12-foot wall. Placing a sofa on the shorter 12-foot wall will square the space, resulting in a room that feels wider instead of long and narrow. Visually, this will make the room feel larger and more proportioned and balanced.

You'll achieve the most benefit by placing as many of the long pieces of furniture as you can parallel to the short walls, priori-tizing the longest pieces first. Here are tricks for some common pieces of furniture:

- *Sofas.* Most studio and one-bedroom apartments have a shorter wall with a window (with an air conditioner unit or a radiator below the window). When that is the case, position your sofa along the window wall so that the back of the couch is parallel to the window. (This means if you sit on the couch, your back would be to the window.) This arrangement has many benefits: The sofa will disguise an unattractive radiator or air conditioner, the window will frame the sofa and the sofa will offer the window area a sense of scale relative to the other furniture in the room. Additionally, if your immediate view when you open the front door to your apartment is the shorter wall (either with or without a window), this setup will present a more interesting focal point when you enter the room.

- *Rectangular tables or desks.* If you are using a rectangular table for your dining area or work space, follow the same approach as you would for a sofa, and place it along one of the shorter walls so that the long side of the table is parallel to the short wall and the short side of the table is parallel to the longer wall. If instead you prefer to determine the location of the dining table based on proximity to the kitchen area and placement of desks based on lighting (a common preference), that approach would work as well.

- *Beds.* People tend to have strong preferences about where to put a bed since a bed serves as the primary comfort and sleeping area. Again, the same principle applies to beds as for sofas and long tables. If you are restricted by space or prefer a particular position for the bed, it will most likely not make or break the balance of the apartment.

Group Furniture Off the Wall

When you visit someone's home, more often than not you will find at least a few pieces of furniture that appear to be aimlessly placed within a room without any regard for how they relate to one another or to the other surrounding objects. Couple this with the natural instinct to push as many objects as close to the wall as possible in an attempt to save space, and now the room feels seriously chaotic. The better approach is to pull your furniture off the wall, and group the pieces closer together based on a similar function.

Think about what you are trying to achieve. If, for instance, you are designing your living room area, you might want to designate one key area as the primary social space. Let's say you are working with a sofa, a coffee table and some chairs. By pulling these pieces closer together in a tight arrangement, you are defining the space as a place for mingling. The seating arrangement is snugger, which changes the circulation path, forcing people to walk around the space rather than through it.

In order to determine where on the floor to position your furniture arrangement, you should go with one of these options:

- Align to a visually attractive and strong element (such as a window or fireplace).

- Align more symmetrically (centered on the wall as opposed to aligned to the far left or far right).

- Pull the furniture to the middle of the room and align with no particular object or element. (Center the furniture between the walls as much as possible.)

If your space doesn't have any strong visual elements or anything that you can properly align to, you don't have to force an alignment. It is not necessary to line things up if you place the emphasis on the furniture arrangement itself.

Avoid Alignment With Peculiarly Placed Windows and Doors

In small spaces, the alignment of doors and windows can sometimes be a bit off. Why? Because smaller apartments are oftentimes the result of being broken off from larger apartments in an attempt to create additional housing. For this reason, and as a general rule, it is best to avoid aligning objects and furniture to areas that are not centered on the wall. For example, if you attempt to align furniture with a window that is off center or at an angle, it will accentuate the asymmetrical position of the window. Instead, de-emphasize the window by creating a furniture composition in a different location.

AIM FOR CONSISTENCY WITH FLOORING OPTIONS

Use one flooring option throughout your space to make the space look larger and balanced. Some of the more common options are discussed here.

Hardwood Flooring and Area Rugs

Hardwood floors are fairly easy surfaces to clean and better for allergies. The flip side is that wood floors are cold and hard on the feet, which is why area rugs can help warm up the floors and soften the surface. However, using area rugs can be tricky. When placed on top of a bare wooden surface, area rugs can create more noticeably separate and distinct floor areas as compared with a surface with wall-to-wall carpeting. Too many rugs can result in visual noise that causes the space to appear smaller, disrupted and less crisp. This effect is accentuated if the rugs are not properly sized, meaning that they appear out of balance with the proportions of the room or the scale of the furniture.

To avoid choppiness when using area rugs, ensure that the area rugs are appropriate in both ratio and scale relative to the furniture. One safe and simple method for sizing a rug is to check whether all of the furniture sits on the carpet, with extra rug space extended equivalently all around. For instance, if you measure the outline of your furniture arrangement to be 8 feet by 10 feet, you should probably get a 9-foot-by-12-foot rug. (Professional designers obtain a higher level of rug-size precision through the use of a floor plan, in which they record all necessary furniture- and floor-space measurements and then illustrate that on a plan that tells them what rug size will work best.)

If you have wooden flooring and would rather not bother with figuring out the correct application of area rugs, then it is probably a better idea to avoid using area rugs altogether so that your floor surface reflects hardwood throughout the entire apartment; this will maintain a flowing, continuous feel.

Wall-to-Wall Carpeting

One of the best flooring options for establishing a sense of continuity and consistency is using the same wall-to-wall carpeting scheme throughout the apartment, from one room or area to the next. The smooth flow works to widen a room's boundaries. Plus, carpeting helps to absorb noise. For strong results, carpeting should be fairly monotone with subtle patterns.

Try a cut-and-loop-knot-style carpet, which, in contrast to plush solid-cut carpeting, will not reflect footprints and dirt. The cut-and-loop-knot-style carpet is flatter (yet no less plush) and thus visually less impressionable. It also reflects the light in an interesting way, giving a two-tone look or appearance.

Carpeting is also especially effective in the sleeping area, where you may want a softer touch.

Wall-to-Wall Carpeting and Area Rugs

As an elegant alternative to using just hardwood floors or wall-to-wall carpeting, you can use a mix-and-match approach by placing an area rug over your carpeting. This distinguishes certain areas, like a bedroom or dining area, while maintaining an even, smooth look all around. Again, the area rug needs to be proportional to the outlined space so that it defines the room as opposed to cutting it off at awkward points. If you have wall-to-wall carpeting in the living room and want to use an area rug to define the conversation area, make sure that the rug fits comfortably beneath the furniture so that the edges of the rug adequately extend beyond the outside perimeter of the furniture arrangement.

Although subject to change, an average or reasonable price range for wall-to-wall carpeting for a 500-square-foot apartment may be between $2,000 and $3,500. If you would like to combine area rugs with wall-to-wall carpeting, an average or reasonable price range would be an additional $500 to $1,200. An average or reasonable price range for area rugs if you have hardwood flooring and nothing else (e.g., no carpeting or rugs) may be between $1,200 and $2,000.

UNDERSTAND YOUR WINDOW TREATMENT OPTIONS

Many people don't give much thought to window treatments — curtains, draperies, blinds, valances, shades — other than for the obvious benefit of being able to block out sunlight and prevent outsiders from looking in. If used properly, however, window treatments can enhance the aesthetics of the apartment by serving as a focal point, framing the windows and highlighting the outside vista. They can also disguise less-attractive views.

A starting point is to determine whether you have an outside view that you would like to accentuate. This will drive your window treatment decision. In all cases, it is important to ensure that the window treatment is proportionate to the scale and size of the windows it surrounds.

Apartments With Attractive Outside Views

For those with strong outside views, such as a park or a skyline, use window treatments to emphasize the view. Framing devices such as side panels (draperies made of fabric that hang to the sides of the window in a stationary fashion) do just that by structuring and defining the window area. This technique also creates a sense of intrigue as to what exists beyond. An effective framing method is to couple side panels with either a valance (decorative drapery) or a cornice board (an ornamental header treatment that sits below the ceiling or within the window frame and extends horizontally across the window's top edge). This will establish a decorative border around the outside view, thus resulting in a stronger visual image with additional focus on that area.

Although subject to change, an average or reasonable price range for a window treatment in instances in which you have a strong outside view may be between $500 and $1,000 for a pre-made arrangement without a header treatment like a valance or cornice board. An average or reasonable price range to add a header treatment may be an additional $500 to $1,500.

Apartments Without Attractive Outside Views

If you do not have an attractive view from your window, downplay the view altogether by selecting an intriguing window treatment that will not only enhance and emphasize the interior of the apartment but also block the view when the window treatment is fully extended or closed. Either a combination of drapery treatments (such as blackout or decorative shades coupled with side panels) or other window treatments that engage the eye (such as vertical blinds) can achieve this objective.

A roman or pleated roman shade made with translucent fabric is one option that allows light to come through while hiding the outside vista. To add decorative effect to a translucent roman shade, you can follow the same approach as above by introducing a cornice board with a pair of side panels; however, in this instance, since the view is blocked by the shade, the addition of a horizontal cornice above the window will serve as a nice header that frames and accentuates the window as an aesthetic entity, thereby shifting the attention away from the outside view. By positioning the cornice over the entire top part of the window frame and ensuring that it extends out 6 to 8 inches on either side of the window frame, you can make the window appear even larger. This option allows the side panels to flank the outer frames of the window instead of resting inside the window frame or over the window itself.

In modern apartments with wider windows that stop at the sill, vertical shades work very well. These tilting blinds offer closure when completely shut or a view when partially or fully opened. They can also be translucent, allowing light to come in while blocking the view.

Although subject to change, an average or reasonable price range for a window treatment in instances in which you do not have an attractive view may be between $3,000 and $5,000.

General Window Treatment Tips

If you have a nice-looking view, you may want to consider combining an approach that not only emphasizes the outside view via a framing device but also looks appealing from the interior. Charming shades or draperies work well for this. For instance, by pairing shades with a pair of side panels, you can create a strong composition that works well as both a framing device and as an interior focal point. For an open and airy feel, sheer draperies or light-colored panels are best. Occasionally modern apartments have a series of windows that extend only halfway up the wall: If this is the case, roman shades with or without short side panels that reach the top of the sill work great. Another helpful strategy is to use horizontal blinds and drapery treatments if the windows are located at the end of a long narrow room, thus emphasizing the breadth of the room.

Although subject to change, an average or reasonable price range for a combination window treatment may be between $2,500 and $4,000.

HANDLE ACCESSORIES WISELY
Display Art as a Grouping

Artwork can cheer up and calm down or brighten and darken the feel of a room. By changing the art, you can influence the room's overall mood and tone.

If artwork is scattered on different walls — and is of varying sizes — the effect will be similar to that of placing disparate pieces of furniture around a room without consideration for how the pieces relate to one another, which produces a sense of clutter.

Conversely, a closely bound art grouping on a wall — similar to a tight-knit seating arrangement — creates a visually strong impact and introduces a sense of clarity and cohesiveness. In addition, this striking composition allows the wall itself to serve as a visual destination and a framing device for the artwork (similar to a picture within a picture). The result is a more engaging design and an overall bolder impression.

This technique works particularly well for grouping smaller-sized works as a unit. For a strong effect, make sure there is not too much or too little open space surrounding the artwork. Artwork is most effectively displayed when the pieces are hung a half-inch apart from one another in all directions. (This is notably important if the works are the same size.) When possible, the frames should match one another and the other finishes in the room, especially if you have furniture or other objects that are polished chrome or matte black. (Those colors are particularly powerful with artwork.)

When placing art, be mindful of surrounding decoration and architecture, as to establish visual continuity within the space. In other words, align the top of an artwork's frame with, say, the top of a door or the bottom of the frame with the top of the light dimmer.

In general, necessary materials for hanging artwork include picture hooks, a hammer, a tape measure and a pencil for marking the spot where to hammer in the nail. Picture hooks, which can be found at any hardware store, should correspond with the weight of the piece that you would like to hang. For instance, if a painting is 2 pounds, then buy a hook that holds a little more weight, like a 5-pound hook. It is important to make sure that the hooks or nails used for hanging artwork are specifically designed for pictures (as indicated on the packaging) as opposed to basic nails, which leave bigger holes in the wall and are generally not as effective. Don't use glue to hang pictures, as glue defaces the wall and could possibly damage the artwork. If you can't balance the hammer in one hand and the picture hook in the other, it means that the hammer is too heavy. Also, try not to hang a picture from its frame because it is likely to fall off the wall or tilt. If it's a particularly heavy work, it might be better to have a professional hang it, as heavier pieces require special assembly and support systems.

As a first step, take inventory of your existing artwork. Determine which pieces have similar attributes (size, shape, appeal, theme, color) and will work well as a group. When purchasing new pieces, pay attention to these characteristics so that you may achieve the best decorative results.

Use Mirrors to Enhance Small Spaces

Mirrors are particularly valuable in small spaces. In addition to having decorative and functional uses, they can enhance lighting, capture unique views, enlarge spaces and add balance to a room. To take advantage of these benefits, it is important to understand how to properly place mirrors and how they can affect your space.

Positioning for optimal appeal. A decorative mirror is most effective when it is proportionate to the wall on which it is placed. This means that, as when positioning artwork, the wall should act as a framing device. Visually, the mirror should be centered with enough wall space around it so that the mirror does not appear too small or too large. For example, if the mirror is 3 feet by 5 feet, the mirror's wall space should be approximately 4 feet by 6 feet or a similar proportion.

When determining how high to hang larger mirrors, take into account the average scale of a person's body. An easy method is to align the bottom of the mirror with your waist and the top so that it extends slightly beyond your head. This means that the bottom generally starts about 3 feet from the floor and spans up to 6 feet high, or within a comfortable range relative to your height. One exception is for dressing mirrors, which usually span from the floor to approximately ceiling height; however, these are best placed on a door of a closet or somewhere more discreet since they are used mostly for functional purposes (such as viewing outfits) rather than for enhancing decor. When determining the height for smaller mirrors (those that reflect only a portion of a person's body, such as the face or torso), place them so that they are equidistant from the sides of the wall and the middle is a bit above eye level.

Adding consistency and embellishment. One effective strategy is to frame your mirror. As with artwork, the frame should relate to the rest of the furnishings in your home. If your furniture has chrome legs or arms, you should use chrome frames. Similarly, if there are hints of black in the room, you should use black frames. By keeping consistent with the theme of the apartment, you can subtly connect the pieces to one another as opposed to introducing a new color or finish that might cause interference.

Correcting a room's imbalance. If a space is noticeably long and narrow — like a hallway — balance the room by positioning a mirror vertically on the wall (so that the mirror's short side is pointing up toward the ceiling). It helps to think of the mirror as running against the grain, opposite the direction of the wall size.

Most mirrors are oval or rectangular (as opposed to square), so there is usually a side that is shorter. The vertical position creates the visual effect of squaring off the space by downplaying the room's length and accentuating its height, thus making it feel more like a room rather than a tunnel.

As a comparison in the same setting, if you were to place a mirror horizontally on the wall (so that the mirror's long side spans across the wall from left to right), the mirror would emphasize the length of the room, thereby resulting in a space that would feel longer and more cramped. For apartments that have dispro-portionately high ceilings, placing a mirror horizontally will tone down the ceiling height and emphasize the length of the room, which will make for a more comfortable and spacious room.

A creative way to use square or circular mirrors is to place them in a series to achieve a horizontal or vertical effect, similar to that of grouping pictures or artwork. In other words, placing four identical square mirrors next to each other on a wall creates a horizontal effect. If you were to take that same series and place it along the wall so that each mirror stood on top of the previous, this arrangement would have a vertical effect.

Capturing light. Using mirrors to reflect and attract natural light from an outside source, or hanging mirrors in the right places, cre-ates the perception of light and space. A simple experiment is to place a mirror across from (or at an angle to) a window so that the mirror reflects the landscape beyond. If done correctly, this should have the dual effect of capturing sunlight as well as the view from outside. If you happen to have a particularly nice view, the effect can be astonishing. This concept can also be used to amplify the light emitted from a sconce or light fixture within your apartment.

Hanging mirrors. The approach for hanging mirrors is very much the same as for hanging artwork, except that mirrors need stronger picture hooks since they tend to be heavier. In addition, because of their weight and fragility, mirrors should never be hung by their frames but rather by the wire that usually comes with the mirror and spans the sides of the mirror frame.

Although subject to change, an average or reasonable price range for (non-recessed) mirrors may be between $250 and $1,250. A key factor influencing this price range is whether the mirror comes with a bevel, which is a decorative detail that consists of a slight slant at the edges of the mirror. The purpose of the bevel is to provide a more decorative look and facilitate the transition between surface levels. Non-bevel mirrors are usually between $250 and $1,000, and mirrors with bevels tend to range between $750 and $1,500. Essentially, mirrors with bevels will increase the cost by approximately 30 percent. In addition, more elaborate wooden frames are more expensive than simple metal ones.

DIY FURNITURE SELECTION AND ARRANGEMENT CHECKLIST
Suggested Steps:

- Determine the key areas that you would like to create or enhance (e.g., dining area, living room area, work space). Take inventory of your space and identify your most pressing needs (e.g., storage, seating, table/desk space, shelves to display a particular collection of art or other specialty items).

- Take note of the first wall that you notice when you open your front door. This area is a major focal point, and you will want to focus your design efforts here. At a minimum, make sure that this wall gives the appearance of being clean and attractive.

- Group your existing furniture elements together according to their function (e.g., coffee tables, desks, chairs, ottomans, lamps).

- Determine the shape of your apartment, and identify the longer walls if your apartment is more rectangular than square.

- Locate anything along the shorter walls that serves as an unattractive focal point (air conditioners or radiators) and which you can disguise with a piece of furniture. Determine whether you have any strong visual attractions along the wall nearest to where you intend to align your furniture.

- Identify your longest pieces of furniture (e.g., sofa, desk, dining table) and experiment with placing those along the shorter walls. Think about factors such as what serves as a better focal point, which pieces better hide less-appealing parts of the shorter walls, which are the longer and more rectangular pieces and which pieces fit better in the space.

- Position the furniture arrangement so that it's off the wall and aligned to either a strong visual attraction or a centered element. If neither of those exists, position your arrangement as close as possible to the middle of the room. Arrange the pieces as close together as you can without allowing them to touch one another.

- When introducing new furniture into your space, focus on selecting pieces that satisfy your immediate needs, and apply the guidance throughout this section to ensure that your pieces are of high quality and have a light and airy feel. Ensure that the color scheme of your furniture is consistent and appropriate throughout.

- Select one flooring option that is most suitable to your needs, and use it consistently throughout your space.

- Determine whether you have an attractive outside view or whether there is anything beyond the window that is personally appealing to you. If you have a view that you would like to accentuate, select window treatments that frame and highlight this view, such as side panels. If you do not have an attractive view from your window, select an intriguing window treatment that will enhance the interior of the apartment and downplay the outside view.

DIY ACCESSORIES CHECKLIST
Suggested Steps:

- Take inventory of your existing artwork, and determine which pieces have similar attributes (size, shape, appeal, theme, color) and will work well as a group. When purchasing new pieces, pay attention to these characteristics so that you may achieve the best decorative results. Position and hang your pieces along a wall of your choosing while ensuring that they are aligned, spaced and grouped properly.

- Determine whether there is a particular view that you would like to accentuate, whether the room is noticeably unbalanced (feels too long or too wide), whether you have a natural source of light that can be leveraged and whether there is a particular wall that lends itself to a mirror. Follow the above guidance to determine how to best use and place mirrors for this particular situation. When purchasing or selecting new mirrors, pay attention to whether the frames match the look and feel of the other items in your apartment.

LIGHTING

Proper light improves the look and feel of any space and allows you to play with the theme of your home. The wrong kind of lighting can make your home appear cold and small and create shadows that darken the room. Choosing a welcoming lighting scheme and using several smaller, warm lamps (rather than bright overhead lighting) will keep the atmosphere friendly. Regardless of room size, creating a cozy space is challenging. For smaller apartments, downlights or architectural lighting may be more appropriate in particular instances, but the use of table or standing lamps will add a layer of intimacy.

UNDERSTAND AMBIENT LIGHTING

In small spaces, it is important to have at least one dominant lighting source that not only serves as the basis for the room's overall lighting but also contributes to the space's atmosphere and mood. This type of general lighting is referred to as ambient lighting.

Start by getting a sense of where the electrical connections are located in your space. Identify where you need the most light, how accessible it will be to turn the light on and off and whether the placement of the light will fit with the existing objects in the space.

Ultimately you should choose an ambient lighting option that supplies the strongest light, provides easy on and off access, makes the best use of space and fits with the theme of the apartment (color, shape, size, feel). Lamps with dimmers also provide the flexibility of controlling the mood and ambience at will — from bright and cheerful to cozy and romantic.

Different types of ambient lights are discussed here:

Table Lamps

When choosing table lamps that act as a primary source of light, it's best to select white or light-colored shades for bright ambient lighting. Also, select lamps that are properly weighted and stable so as to avoid fixtures that can easily topple and subsequently break. The lamp's base should be wide and heavy to maintain balance. As with all ambient lighting sources, it is helpful to select a lamp that can accommodate LED bulbs equivalent to 100 watts or greater.

Floor Lamps

The key with floor lamps is to ensure that the top allows light to be projected in a far-ranging, 360-degree radius. That is why you can achieve wonders by selecting a floor lamp with a large all-white or clear glass dome top. In general, fixtures with glass shades provide better overall lighting, whereas metal shades are better suited for decorative purposes. If a floor lamp's top is made of metal or a dark fabric, the flow of light will be restricted — a result of the light not being able to pass through. This is generally the case with torchieres (*torch lamps*), which are tall floor lamps with partially covered, non-translucent, bowl-shaped metal tops that primarily cast light in one direction, depending on positioning. That makes the lamp less effective as a primary lighting source (unless your goal is to specifically direct light toward the floor or ceiling).

Standing Tube Lamps

In contrast to other tall and narrow fixtures that disperse light from only the top of the stem, standing tube light lamps are essentially long, hollow, cylindrical-shaped lamps that extend vertically from the floor and disseminate light from top to bottom and on all sides. They work well in living room spaces to fill the apartment with light and provide a luminous overall glow. They save on space because they are narrow (8 to 12 inches in diameter) and allow for light to span 360 degrees in a range of approximately 6 feet in all directions.

Pendants

Pendants are light fixtures that are suspended from the ceiling by cords, chains or rods. They are a form of overhead lighting that tends to function as task lighting, since they are positioned to focus primarily on what lies directly beneath them. A dining pendant, for instance, directs a focused light toward the dining table over which the pendant hangs. Dining pendant beams tend to be narrow, spreading from one end of a table to the other. If the pendants are globe-shaped, they can provide additional but limited ambient lighting. In contrast to chandeliers, which have a wide range of light, pendants create a more focused light source. (Although in general, the closer the pendant is to the ceiling, the more widespread the light will be.) They are also less fussy and more streamlined than a chandelier, which can sometimes overwhelm a space if it has too many arms and decorative elements.

Sconces

Sconces are decorative fixtures that are positioned on a wall. They provide powerful multidirectional ambient lighting and are a great solution for those who don't have electrical capabilities in the ceiling. Sconces are best installed at a height of approximately 66 inches above the floor. For the brightest lighting, it is best to find a high-wattage sconce made of clear or white glass set on a dimmer. If your space doesn't already have a sconce installed on the wall, then this will require a small installation. See Install Sconces for Decorative Ambient Lighting and Space-Saving Capabilities for additional information.

USE TASK LIGHTING TO DISTINGUISH AND DEFINE PARTICULAR AREAS

Task lighting, as the name suggests, refers to lighting that is used to facilitate particular tasks, such as reading or dining. This kind of lighting is commonly achieved by smaller downlights (lights that are designed to project light downward and typically embedded in a ceiling), picture lights (a small lamp positioned over a picture), reading lamps or similar fixtures that emit constricted ranges of light. For smaller apartments, this type of lighting can be creatively used to help break up the space and highlight distinct and separate areas of a room. Using narrow beams of light, task lighting can better define each area's function (working, cooking, relaxing) by assigning different zones within a room. So, while a room may be open without any separating walls that distinguish different areas, the lighting can be used to represent distinct spaces for separate activities through a targeted lighting scheme.

Task lighting works best when it's coupled with ambient lighting, whereby there is one primary lighting source for general lighting and multiple sources for task lighting to further delineate the space. An example of a lighting scheme within a small space might be an ambient overhead light centered on the ceiling for general lighting, downlights over the kitchen counter to define the kitchen space, a pendant over the dining table to define the dining room, a desk lamp on a desk to define a work space or a picture light on a wall that projects light onto artwork below or into the broader space to define the living room.

To influence the mood, energy or ambience, other creative techniques like dimmers can be thrown into the mix.

To come up with an ambient lighting and task-lighting scheme, determine the activities that are most essential or common to your lifestyle: sleeping, eating, working, lounging. Identify what parts of the room are most conducive to these activities and how the existing layout and furniture arrangement can be leveraged. (For example, have you already defined particular spaces using your furniture, or will you have to move things around to define a new space?) Once you have established a zone that accommodates a particular activity, select a lighting fixture that fits with the theme and feel of that particular space. (See Pay Attention to Furniture Arrangement for additional information on creating spaces.)

TAKE ADVANTAGE OF ELECTRICAL CAPABILITIES IN THE CEILING

Most small apartments do not have easily accessible electrical capabilities in the ceiling, so if you have an electrical connection (an outlet) in the ceiling, don't ignore it. This electrical source provides the flexibility for installing ceiling-mounted fixtures or partial ceiling-mounted fixtures (fixtures that are slightly suspended about 6 to 12 inches from the ceiling). These fixtures, which serve as ideal sources for overall lighting, single-handedly provide a comprehensive and adequate amount of light in a room with the flip of a switch, which is a huge benefit. The fixture selection will depend primarily on the size of the room, where the electrical source is located and the existing theme that has been established for the apartment. These fixtures save precious space by eliminating the need for several other lighting sources. Contact your building's superintendent to help identify someone who can assist you with the installation. See Install Sconces for Decorative Ambient Lighting and Space-Saving Capabilities for additional information on installation costs.

DIY LIGHTING CHECKLIST
Suggested Steps:

- Figure out the most convenient location for your primary source of light by getting a sense of where the electrical connections are located, ease of accessibility in terms of turning the light on and off and how the placement of the light fits with the theme of the apartment (color, shape, size, feel).

- Once you have established a "zone" that accommodates a particular activity, determine what lighting fixtures (sconces, floor lamps, ceiling fixtures, pendant lamps, table lamps, etc.) fit with the theme and feel of that particular space.

- Create your lighting scheme. If using lamps, ensure they are properly weighted and stable and have white or clear shades made of glass or fabric. Dimmers are an added benefit.

- If you have an electrical source in the ceiling, select a ceiling-mounted fixture based on the tips throughout this guide.

- For any installation work associated with your lighting selections, identify someone who can assist with the installation. It might help to start with asking the retailer where you purchase your item whether it offers this service. If not, your building's superintendent or manager might know someone.

WITH A DESIGNER

This section refers to projects in which the desired changes are pursued with the help of a professional's expertise and experience. The interior designer functions as a subject-matter expert who assists clients with making the right selections and serves as a guide for helping clients better understand the big picture and make smart decisions.

Here, the primary focus is on soft furnishings (furniture and accessories) without construction or the use of an architect or contractor. These projects are usually not too complicated, yet the overall result is notably unique, impressive and customized to fit the needs and preferences of the client. Interior designers are able to draw upon their knowledge to provide clients with options, solutions and information that would not otherwise be available. A designer can educate clients on how to invest in pieces rather than blindly selecting them. By focusing on problem solving and identifying clever solutions to a client's needs, a good designer will assist in prioritizing preferences, minimizing the required effort and making financially savvy decisions.

For example, a client may want to choose a paint color but then will work with a designer to understand the best application (which walls to paint) or how the color will appear in his or her home since the color reflected on the sample chip may look different when applied to a larger surface. Likewise, a client may look to enhance his or her lighting by choosing lamps but then seek further assistance with selecting and positioning the correct downlights or with obtaining a better understanding of how each type of lighting affects the space. Through a team approach, the client and the designer work together to achieve the client's goals and incorporate critical and overlooked design concepts, such as consistency, definition, proportion, balance and scale.

The use of a professional often comes into play when a person is passionate about an idea or a vision and seeks assurance over the outcome. With the assistance of a designer, a client gets guidance as to how to implement his or her designs and ideas with the additional layer of security that expectations will be met, if not exceeded. Although working with a designer tends to cost more on the surface, designers often have access to better-quality materials and services through their contacts in the industry, as well as trade discounts that they can pass on to their clients, thus saving money on higher-cost items.

However, as with most services and products, not all designers are created equal, and it takes time to find the right fit. The biggest downside of using a designer is the process of selecting whom to use. The designer-client relationship is a partnership, and, like any effective team, this requires collaboration and a sense of trust. If clients are not comfortable with their designer, the project is not likely to succeed. Depending on the designer, there is also the chance that the client's vision will not be accurately captured. If this turns out to be the case, then additional time and money are at stake.

PRICING STRUCTURE

Although prices are subject to change and depend on the interior designer, an average or reasonable price range for professional services relating to the areas discussed in this guide may be between $2,000 and $4,500. This cost accounts for an initial one- to two-hour consultation with a high-end designer (costing approximately $125 to $300) and an additional 20 to 30 hours of the designer's time (at an hourly rate between $125 and $250), during which time the designer advises, plans and consults on furniture placement, color, furniture selection, space and lighting. This price range does not include the costs associated with materials or *construction, which are discussed in this guide as part of each individual tip. As an alternative, if you require only consultation on specific areas, many professionals offer design packages or plans that allow you to select from a variety of options to best suit your needs. These can range from $500 to $10,000 each, depending on the offering.*

Most interior designers have a few different ways in which they charge for their services, including:

- Charging an hourly rate

- Charging an overall-design fee

- Charging for shopping time

- Charging on commission

On average, hourly fees range between $125 and $250 per hour. In an overall-design fee structure, the designer charges a "per room" fee (or a "per project" fee) for developing the overall design, style, theme and floor plan of a room, apartment or house. This fee usually covers the furniture plan or the furniture plan plus development, evolvement and administration of all ideas and purchase orders. The services that are included will be determined based on a discussion with the designer. This structure works well for projects involving a complete revamp of the apartment. In this scenario, a designer can charge as little as $125 for a one-time consultation (or a $1,000 to $1,500 design fee per room) or as much as $2,500 to $10,000 as a design fee for the whole apartment (250 to 900 square feet). Some designers choose to charge an additional shopping fee, which is an hourly charge for visiting showrooms and other locations to shop for, or with, their clients. This charge can range from $50 to $250 per hour and averages between $1,000 and $1,500 per day for travel time if the apartment is located out of town or beyond a 10-mile radius.

Commission-Based Fee Structure Explained

In addition to the above fees, designers can use a commission-based fee structure in instances in which the client is expected to purchase goods. This method is very common and requires further explanation. As members of the interior design profession, designers get a trade or "showroom" discount, which is a percentage discount off the retail (or *list*) price that the general public might pay at a retail store, such as New York City's Gracious Home or Bloomingdales. The size of the discount often depends on the type of good that will be purchased and the vendor that will be used. There are essentially three types of venues from which a designer can purchase furniture at discounted prices:

- *Trade showrooms.* Showrooms can be retail (dealing with the public) but are generally trade oriented (dealing with professionals). Professional interior designers get discounts from the trade showrooms but generally not from public showrooms (retail stores). The general public does not get a discount at trade showrooms. In most cases, trade showrooms offer designers around 25 to 40 percent off of the price when they purchase from the showroom.

- *Antique stores.* Most showrooms don't sell antiques, so these have to be obtained directly from antique stores, which are general retail shops that provide antiques. Antiques are priced differently than the reproductions found in most showrooms. For the most part, anyone can buy from an antique store, but designers get discounts, whereas the public usually does not. Usually, designers can get a 5 to 20 percent discount, which is a smaller discount than they get for the reproduction furniture from trade showrooms.

- *Retail stores/online stores.* General retail shopping — including online shopping — usually does not provide professionals with attractive trade discounts (if any). Occasionally, designers will be offered discounts from retail stores, like Crate and Barrel, but the discounts are usually insignificant. Although there is not much benefit for designers to purchase from retail stores, a designer may purchase goods from a retail store if it happens to carry items that are preferred by the client, dictated by the client's budget or not otherwise available. Other times, a client may request the help of a designer in choosing a product at a particular retail store.

In all instances in which a discount is provided to a designer, the designer is able to transfer the discount to the client. In other words, by working through a designer to assist with purchasing merchandise, the client is able to obtain a wholesale (or *net*) price as opposed to the retail (or *list*) price. The designer then makes a profit by adding a commission on top of the passed-down discount. The commission is based on the price of the item. For instance, if an item sells for $1,000 in a trade showroom or store, designers can get the same item for about $700, which they can then offer to their client for $700 plus a 35 percent or so commission, which includes the design fees in this same cost.

The primary benefit of a commission-based fee structure is that the client is able to get merchandise at a discounted price *and* the added value of a designer's services, which all together can amount to less than the cost that a client might incur if he or she selected and purchased an item alone using retail prices. A designer has resources that are not available or open to the public, which allows for access to unusual and unique custom types of goods and materials. As part of the commission cost, a client gets the advantage of a designer's detailed research and knowledge relating to specialty items and sources. This option is helpful in instances in which the client is looking for specific or custom items that are unique to the apartment and design vision, such as custom pieces from vendors that specialize in specific styles or periods that fit the client's needs. In addition, knowledge about vendors that make one-of-a-kind pieces or that use materials that are rare and distinctive is an added benefit. Those are often the types of pieces and materials that make a home special.

The following advice offers many specific examples of the types of services a designer can provide.

The price information provided herein is for reference purposes only and is based on New York City estimates. Although the author has made every attempt to provide price information that is representative, the prices noted below are intended to reflect the author's viewpoint on what is an expected or reasonable cost for addressing the relevant tip or technique while also keeping true to the specific objectives and quality standards expressed in this guide. The actual price will depend on a variety of factors, including the quality of service/materials, location, the current market and the scope of work.

COLOR AND PAINT

When choosing what to do with the walls in your apartment, it's a smart idea to connect with a professional to figure out what will work best for your specific space. There are many horror stories that could have been quite easily prevented through simple pre-cautions. For example, one client who opted not to use a designer to assist with selecting a paint color picked a shade of light pink from a display of small chips at a retail paint store. When applied to the dining room wall, the resulting color was a garish hot pink.

Meanwhile, paint isn't the only way to add color to the walls. Wallpaper can camouflage a wall's current wear and tear, and it is also effective for safeguarding a wall's surface. The same goes for fabric and tile. With the help of an interior designer, there are many crafty ways that color can be used to enhance a space.

USE COLOR TO CREATE VISUAL TRICKS

Color can be used to make a space look bigger, define interior areas and visually correct a room's size imbalance. The following examples show how.

Define Space Through This Simple Color Technique

Imagine standing in the middle of a square room with white walls. In front of you is a living room area for relaxing. Directly behind you is a dining room area for eating. To define the relaxing and eating spaces, imagine painting a line through the center of the room and painting the entire living room space gray. Now you have one full wall that's gray, one full wall that's white and two walls that are half gray and half white. Without building any walls, you have effectively defined your living room and dining room spaces with the use of color.

This technique is extremely effective to distinguish functional areas that are in close proximity to each other in small apartments. This method can be used with paint, wallpaper, tile (tile is usually best for bathrooms and kitchens) or upholstered fabric (if you want to get creative). If, for instance, the eating area is in a tiny corner of your apartment, you can apply paint or wallpaper so that the boundaries of your eating space are defined by the color that you choose.

Change Proportions Through Visually Manipulating Ceiling Height

In general, studio apartments tend to be long and narrow with the ceilings feeling either too low or too high. The ideal situation is to have a space that is more squared as opposed to narrow. This is less common for studio apartments; however, even when the space is more squared, you may also feel that the ceiling is too high or too low. To correct for these types of imbalances and alter the perception of size and shape, designers can employ a variety of color techniques. Some of the more effective strategies involve the use of darker and warmer colors or lighter and cooler colors. You learned earlier (see Select the Right Paint Color) that darker and warmer colors make spaces feel cozier and more intimate, and lighter and cooler colors make spaces feel more spacious and calm. One additional related effect is that darker and warmer colors can visually shrink a space, and lighter and cooler colors can visually expand a space.

Suppose that you have a square-shaped room that's painted all light blue, but the ceiling feels too high. By painting the ceiling a darker and warmer shade of blue (while keeping all other things constant), you can visually bring the ceiling height down, thus making the ceiling feel closer to you. If this same space were painted all blue and the ceiling felt too low, you could paint the ceiling a lighter and cooler shade of blue to visually raise the ceiling height, thus making the ceiling feel farther away from you.

It gets trickier once you begin to introduce more variables, such as different colors versus different shades, but here are some simplified examples of strategies that designers can employ in square spaces:

For SQUARE spaces where the ceiling feels too high (how to visually lower the ceiling height)	For SQUARE spaces where the ceiling feels too low (how to visually raise the ceiling height)
• Paint the *Ceiling* a darker and warmer color than all the walls below	• Paint the *Ceiling* a lighter and cooler color than all the walls below

In narrow, longish spaces, the same concepts work for the ceiling. However, depending on the extent of the narrowness, you may also want to further visually widen the walls so that the space feels more balanced:

For **NARROW** spaces where the ceiling feels too high (how to visually lower the ceiling height and widen the walls)	For **NARROW** spaces where the ceiling feels too low (how to visually raise the ceiling height and widen the walls)
• Paint the *Ceiling* a darker and warmer color than all the walls below; **OR**	• Paint the *Ceiling* a lighter and cooler color than all the walls below; **OR**
• Paint the *Ceiling* and the *Shorter Walls* a darker and warmer color than the longer walls. The longer walls should be a lighter and cooler color relative to the ceiling and shorter walls. To keep things simple, the same color should be used for the ceiling and the shorter walls; **OR**	• Paint the *Ceiling* and the *Longer Walls* a lighter and cooler color than the shorter walls. The shorter walls should be a darker and warmer color relative to the ceiling and shorter walls. To keep things simple, the same color should be used for the ceiling and the longer walls; **OR**
• Paint the *Ceiling* and *One Shorter Wall* a darker and warmer color than all other walls. To keep things simple, the same color should be used for the ceiling and the shorter wall.	• Paint the *Ceiling* and *All Walls* a lighter and cooler color than the current color of the ceiling and walls. To keep things simple, the same color should be used for the ceiling and all walls.

One interesting effect of painting the walls and the ceiling the same color is that your eye will register the space as one continuous surface with no definite beginning or end, so in essence this amplifies the effect that you are going for, whether it be to open the space or make it feel more cozy.

A similar concept applies in spaces that have moldings at chair-rail height (usually prewar apartments):

For **SQUARE** spaces where the ceiling feels too high (how to visually lower the ceiling height)	For **SQUARE** spaces where the ceiling feels too low (how to visually raise the ceiling height)
• Paint the *Molding* plus the *Space Above The Molding* (*Ceiling* plus *Molding* plus the *Wall Space Above The Molding*) a darker and warmer color than all other spaces. To keep things simple, the same color should be used for the molding plus the space above the molding.	• Paint the *Molding* plus the *Space Above The Molding* (*Ceiling* plus *Molding* plus the *Wall Space Above The Molding*) the same lighter and cooler color as all other spaces. To keep things simple, the same color should be used for the molding plus the space above the molding.
For NARROW spaces where the ceiling feels too high (how to visually lower the ceiling height and widen the walls)	**For NARROW spaces where the ceiling feels too low (how to visually raise the ceiling height and widen the walls)**
• Paint the *Molding* plus the *Space Above The Molding* (*Ceiling* plus *Molding* plus the *Wall Space Above The Molding*) a darker and warmer color than all other spaces. To keep things simple, the same color should be used for the molding plus the space above the molding.	• Paint the *Molding* plus the *Space Above The Molding* (*Ceiling* plus *Molding* plus the *Wall Space Above The Molding*) a lighter and cooler color than all other spaces. To keep things simple, the same color should be used for the molding plus the space above the molding.

At a basic level, wall moldings are wooden, plaster, plastic or stone enhancements applied horizontally throughout the interior of the room. They are usually placed at chair-rail height (between approximately 24 inches and 36 inches from the floor) or just below the ceiling at picture height (between approximately 1 inch and 5 inches from the ceiling). Moldings are both functional and aesthetic: They not only protect the wall from contact with furniture (like rubbing from the backs of chairs) but also add scale and proportion to a room and serve as a resting place for the eye. Picture moldings originally existed for the purpose of providing a rail on which to hang paintings. In bigger spaces, moldings are painted a contrast color for purposeful emphasis; however, that's not a particularly effective technique in smaller spaces as it can result in distraction. Note that for moldings other than those at chair-rail height (such as picture moldings), it often works best to follow the general color rules indicated in the first two charts and to paint the moldings the same color as the walls (as if the moldings didn't exist).

It is also important to understand that since moldings are oftentimes made of wood, they require a satin finish, which is slightly glossy, so the finish level of the molding will further differentiate it from the wall color but not so much that it breaks up the continuity of the space, as the glossiness will be very subtle.

See Paint Application Basics for price information regarding painting.

USE WALLPAPER, TILES AND FABRIC

Like with paint, the use of wallpaper, tiles and fabric can add variation and texture to a surface area while also establishing distinct spaces. These materials follow the same color rules as paint.

For instance, when darker and warmer wallpaper, tile or fabric is placed below a molding at chair-rail height and the wall directly above the wallpaper is painted a lighter and cooler color, the space will be visually divided from top to bottom and feel more expansive. This will also provide a cozy feeling to the space below the chair rail — usually the height where relaxation activities such as sitting, lounging and sleeping are performed.

Conversely, when lighter and cooler paint is applied below a molding at chair-rail height and darker and warmer wallpaper, tile or fabric is applied above chair-rail height, the room may feel closer together, as if the walls were encroaching on the space above the chair rail.

Although wallpaper, tile and fabric can be more costly (due to costs associated with purchasing the materials, prepping the walls and installation), you can save a significant amount in the long run by hiding wall imperfections and protecting against further nicks and scratches.

Although subject to change, an average or reasonable price range for non-paint materials (wallpaper, tiles, fabric) for walls within a 500-square-foot apartment (the assumption is that you will apply the material to only some walls and to only parts of the walls) may be between $250 and $1,000. The application of the material (labor), which consists of prepping the wall to accept the selected material and then applying it to the surface area, will be an additional cost and may be between $800 and $1,200.

CONSIDER UNUSUAL PAINT APPLICATIONS AND TECHNIQUES

Fashion is a prime example of expression and individualism. Clothes and accessories make a statement, and there are endless options for distinguishing yourself and having fun. Similarly, there are numerous paint applications and techniques that can provide your home with a unique and appealing look. But there's a costly difference between fashion and interior design: If you buy an outfit you don't like, you can return it, whereas interior design is a more

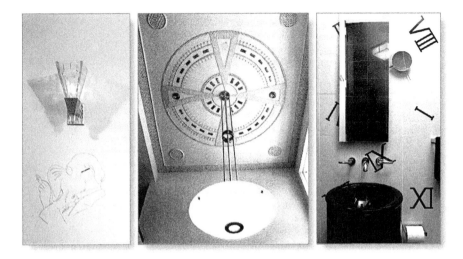

permanent expression. That's why it's important to get your space right the first time. A designer and a painter can work together to implement any creative idea that you may have (or develop one for you) in a manner that ensures that the overall design scheme is proportional and balanced while also thematically interesting and appropriate. Here are a few examples:

Venetian Plaster

Used on walls and ceilings, Venetian plaster is an elegant, high-end interior finish that first became popular in Venice, Italy, because of its durability and attractiveness. Venetian plaster consists of several layers of plaster — one upon another — resulting in a thick, glossy and smooth finish that is resistant to dents and scratches. Because of the intricacies of its application, the plaster provides a visually varied appearance while also giving the wall a sense of depth. This technique evokes a feeling of sophistication and movement. Its resilient and easy-to-clean surface also works miracles in high-traffic areas or areas that might be prone to getting wet, such as kitchens and bathrooms. The living and dining room areas are also excellent places to experiment with Venetian plaster if you are going for a luxe impression.

Because the creation and application of Venetian plaster can be quite complex, it is usually best to engage a professional decorative painter to perform the work for you. Regular house painters are generally not qualified or trained in this technique, which involves mixing plaster, color pigmentation and other ingredients such as dust and marble and then applying the mixture to a wall surface with a spatula-like utensil, similar to the application of exterior stucco.

Although subject to change, an average or reasonable price range for Venetian plaster (materials and service costs — excluding interior design fees) for approximately 150 square feet of coverage (a wall that is about 10 feet high and 15 feet long) may be between $2,200 and $3,000. This includes application of the plaster and primer by a professional decorative painter, a custom sample for the client to approve and insurance against surface damage. Prices for materials tend to range from $5 to $20 per square foot based on the current conditions of the walls and the complexity of the finish. The cost is influenced by the number of coats. The more coats of plaster, the more expensive, but the more coats that are added, the more depth and beauty is created.

Ragging, Sponging and Striae

These cost-effective painting methods give your space interest, depth and drama. Ragging (or *rag painting*) uses thinned paint mixed with glaze and is applied with a cloth to give the wall surface an animated and energetic texture. Similarly, sponging involves the use of sponges to alter the textural design of your wall to introduce depth and shadow. A striae technique uses consistent vertical lines to produce a striped effect that allows ceilings and walls to look higher and thus rooms to appear taller. This works great in rooms with low ceilings. The benefit of these approaches is that you can achieve highly sophisticated-looking designs in a relatively short period of time. All three techniques can enhance your home by adding artistic interest while detracting from wall imperfections.

Although subject to change, an average or reasonable price range for ragging, sponging and striae techniques (materials and service costs — excluding interior design fees) for approximately 150 square feet of coverage (a wall that is about 10 feet high and 15 feet long) may be between $2,000 and $3,000.

Drawings and Illustrations

Scribing (or *wall drawing*) refers to a highly decorative form of writing or drawing (usually with charcoal) on a wall surface to produce a visually appealing and artistic image. You can play with this technique through words, pictures or artistic compositions applied directly to the wall. By creating whimsical, ingenious and original works that introduce creative points of interest, the wall can become a work of art that enhances and defines the room. Murals work in very much the same way except that they are usually created with paint and involve incorporating the architectural elements of the space directly into the artwork in a clever way. To create an interesting drawing or composition for your wall or ceiling, you need to retain an artist or decorative painter. To create a wall mural, which is much more complicated than scribing, you need to retain a trompe l'oeil painter who specializes in these complicated renditions of landscapes, architectural elements and pictorial scenes. The murals will visually simulate a realistic scenario. For instance, if you want to create a niche without really building one, a trompe l'oeil artist can paint one to look as though it exists by cleverly simulating all the details of an authentic niche.

Although subject to change, an average or reasonable price range for scribing may be between $500 and $1,500 for approximately 150 square feet of coverage. For a mural, a starting price may be between $1,000 and $5,000, depending on the expertise of the artist and the difficulty or originality of the design being painted. The lower end of this price range is for less complex designs created by an artist with average expertise.

KEY BENEFITS OF USING A DESIGNER TO ASSIST WITH COLOR AND PAINT

Professional designers can achieve greater results by:

- Implementing a customized, unique and professional color scheme that accurately fits with the size, location, direction, theme, style and shape of your space.

- Recommending color and wall treatments that create and define smaller areas within one larger space.

- Leveraging effective techniques for making the space feel larger and more spacious.

- Producing a sense of variety, interest and color differentiation.

- Offering guidance for maintaining wall surfaces and camouflaging cracks and imperfections.

- Introducing artistic intrigue and beauty to your home in a cost-effective manner.

FURNITURE SELECTION AND ARRANGEMENT

In a small space, furniture is one of the most important home-related investments: A small space accommodates less furniture, so the furniture will have a bigger impact.

LEVERAGE THE EXPERTISE OF AN INTERIOR DESIGNER TO HELP YOU INVEST IN FURNITURE

You should invest in high-quality pieces so that your furniture can outlive your apartment as you move from space to space. This is why it pays to work with an interior designer from the start of your home-design process. Even a one-time consultation can provide valuable insight that you can use to design your home and drive future decisions. If you select the right furniture, you will be setting the path for accumulating quality items that can remain with you for a lifetime. Designers are qualified to advise on critical decisions relating to furniture selection.

Quality Matters

It's particularly important to accumulate furnishings that are high quality and durable. The last thing that you want is to purchase pieces that will appear worn and tired after a few months. Furniture, like financial assets, is an investment that, if chosen

properly, will save you money. Often overlooked but important
considerations that contribute to quality:

- Expected life span or shelf life

- Ease and cost of replacing particular parts

- Effort involved with cleaning and maintaining

- Attractiveness of the warranty

- Transferability and compatibility (how easily a particular
  item can fit with other pieces)

A good designer incorporates these elements into decisions
and has access to — or can direct you to — quality pieces that are
capable of lasting through several homes. In today's market, where
there are low barriers to entry and endless options, it is exceedingly
challenging for the average person to distinguish whether it's worth
investing in that dresser secured by glue or spending a little more
and getting one put together with more permanent materials. The
difference between *investing* in furniture and *selecting* furniture lies
in the ability to look beyond the cosmetic appeal. A good professional
will either directly obtain these pieces for you or educate you on
where to find them. Either way, this knowledge is invaluable since
it can save you significant time, money and angst.

Fabric Colors Can Be Deceiving

Professional designers can implement a design that accounts for
how fabric colors react to different times of the day and how they

relate to the surrounding elements, such as window coverings, the shape of the furniture pieces or the fabrics of other furniture pieces in the room. When selecting particular fabrics, each color should harmoniously blend together without creating a visual disturbance. This doesn't mean that you have to use the same exact shade of blue from piece to piece, but it does mean that the tones of blue selected should relate well to one another.

Planning and Budgeting

Smart decisions stem from a strong plan. A design plan can help you identify and prioritize your needs while maximizing potential benefits. Working with a professional designer, you can assemble a plan that details your preferences, focuses on your most important and immediate needs, fits within your budget and adheres to a realistic timeline. Designers think about space from the point of view of a coherent and consistent floor plan in which they can map out your space functionally, thematically and aesthetically to select the pieces that are right for you.

In addition to developing a well-functioning scheme, a designer can show you how to implement your design in proper phases based on your immediate needs if you do not have the cash reserves to make all purchases in one shot. This type of planning and prioritizing will determine which selections can be made together and which pieces should be obtained at a later date. The planning and budgeting process is not just about the selection of new pieces but also about employing creative problem-solving techniques and experimenting with the space to leverage what you already have. This approach allows you to optimize your spending and focus on what's most critical and necessary.

Scale, Proportion and Balance

Each furniture piece should be viewed as an important part in a puzzle. You may find the sofa of your dreams, but if it doesn't fit correctly within the room or if it makes the surrounding objects look worse (or if you can't even get it through your front door or in the elevator!), it can turn into a nightmare. For example, if you buy a couch that is too large for the space, the couch will overwhelm the room. In addition, the couch may stifle circulation if you're not able to comfortably walk around it.

A professional designer is trained to ensure that each element in a room fits the space and is located within proper relation to neighboring elements. A designer's knowledge of scale, proportion and balance allows for a selection process that results in the best use of your space. This ability requires special attention to measurement, spacing, alignment, relation and theme.

Specialty Furniture

A professional designer has additional resources, such as select vendors, from which the designer can purchase items that cannot be found in the open marketplace. Many of these pieces are specialty items and accessories that are unique, like multifunctioning pieces that are lifesavers in an urban dwelling. For example, a designer can help you find or design versatile pieces of furniture like beds that turn into sofas, tables that rise up and fold down or bookcases that easily appear and disappear. Be sure to leverage an interior designer's ability to obtain rare items, custom pieces and high-quality hardware: In addition to enhancing your home with a fresh and unique appearance, these specialty items are vital if you are looking for complicated or custom furniture with dual purposes that can maintain an elegant and chic feel.

Although costs will vary greatly depending on the type of furniture, the number of pieces, the complexity of customization and the availability of the item(s), among other things, an average or reasonable amount to spend on specialty furniture (materials and service costs — excluding interior design fees) for a 500-square-foot apartment may be between $500 and $4,000.

USE A DESIGNER TO HELP YOU UNDERSTAND HOW TO ARRANGE YOUR FURNITURE

Arranging furniture may seem like a simple exercise, but a professional interior designer's deeper knowledge of more complex concepts, such as spatial relationships, circulation, direction, balance and flow, is the key that ties everything together and transforms a room into a harmonious, artistic design.

The ability to create effective and distinct yet unclosed spaces takes great skill and experience. Establishing proper circulation in a studio or one-bedroom apartment can be complicated because the lack of boundaries can overwhelm furniture. Boundaries are important for helping to define space. Furniture pieces that are thoughtlessly strewn about without consideration for how the pieces relate to one another (e.g., through function, aesthetics or positioning) can result in a space with awkward traffic patterns and disconnected relationships.

An essential component of establishing a strong design pattern is ensuring that separate functional areas flow smoothly into each other. For instance, the living room area should flow seamlessly into the dining area, and the dining area should flow into the kitchen. The resulting flow from space to space and between the walls and furniture has a significant impact on the apartment's overall feel. Interior designers are trained to understand the scale and proportion of a space and can provide valuable knowledge regarding the relationship of furniture selections as well as how different pieces relate to other parts of the apartment, such as neighboring rooms.

FOCUS ON FLOW BETWEEN THE ARCHITECTURE AND THE FURNISHINGS

Good design requires an understanding of spatial relationships. This involves knowing how the inside of the space relates to its exterior, whether that means how the apartment relates to the surrounding landscape or how the furnished interiors relate to the walls. A smooth flow from one room or area to another and between the walls and furniture is very important. Through the creation of a design plan, interior designers can help establish the flow between the furnishings and the space's architecture and design a space that evokes positive energy (yes, energy). Floor plans arguably have more to do with how a space feels rather than how it looks. Once the plan is created, the selection of furniture and finishes will dictate the results. Understated elegance is the cornerstone of effective design. With no one element overriding the next, the furnishings should act in harmony, creating a balance and order. When you walk through a room with good flow, it should evoke a positive feeling. Like the bespoke suit that seems to be perfectly draped upon the body, well-composed plans achieve the same effect: they feel natural, as though they have always existed in time, with a sense of history preserved. Figuring out how to parlay a well-designed plan into action is the professional's job. This task is difficult because unless end users can physically traverse the space, they often can't understand what it will feel like.

KEY BENEFITS OF USING A DESIGNER FOR FURNITURE SELECTION AND ARRANGEMENT
Professional designers can achieve greater results by:

- Ensuring that aesthetically pleasing relationships exist between the furniture and other elements in the apartment.

- Offering valuable insight into complex design concepts such as circulation, balance and flow.

- Establishing an appropriate color scheme for furniture that takes into account important variables such as the time of day, the relationship to surrounding elements, the shape of furniture pieces and the effect of furniture coverings.

- Selecting high-quality pieces that maintain their value and appearance over longer periods of time and have a higher degree of compatibility with other objects.

- Providing budgeting and planning guidance, including assistance with prioritizing preferences and minimizing spending.

- Applying specialized knowledge about scale, proportion and balance to help ensure that the selection process results in the best fit for your space.

- Obtaining rare items, custom pieces and high-quality hardware that adds functionality and exclusivity to your home.

LIGHTING

A designer can be instrumental in helping you to select, obtain and install a customized, complicated or unique lighting scheme. The best lighting option will depend on the attributes of your existing space as well as the effect that you are looking to achieve. At a minimum, it pays to consult with a designer to understand your options and decide on a direction that fits with your budget and preferences. Although you can select sconces and track lighting on your own, it may be wiser to team with a designer to properly identify a qualified individual for the installation as well as have the designer provide that person with proper instructions. For example, the average person might not know that sconces should generally be installed at slightly above eye level, where the junction box can be centered. For this reason, some sconces may look awkward with low ceiling walls, narrow passageways or other spaces with less room. For track lighting, a designer can assist you with locating the track and positioning the corresponding heads so that your space is lit correctly. If you desire to install downlights, you will need to know how they should be positioned if you want them to operate most effectively. Simply placing downlights 6 or 8 inches apart does very little to create effective lighting patterns. Artwork lighting, meanwhile, is quite complex and requires the services of a professional who can both specify and locate these specialized fixtures.

If you are looking to get a bit fancier, you can work with a designer to draw up a plan that illustrates the suggested placement of light fixtures and receptacles for the ceiling. This will provide a high-level overview of how much lighting there will be as well as the types of lighting that will be used throughout the apartment. This is great if you want a sense for how the space will look when everything is complete. Other helpful considerations include the positioning of soffits for downlights and selecting the correct cans in relation to the furnishings.

See Lighting for price information regarding lighting schemes.

KEY BENEFITS OF USING A DESIGNER FOR LIGHTING DECISIONS
Professional designers can achieve greater results by:

- Establishing customized, task-specific, complicated and unique lighting schemes that are not otherwise attainable.

- Informing you about lighting options that are available for your space as well as the factors that drive those options.

SMALL RENOVATIONS

For these types of projects, clients can discuss their ideas or questions with either a professional designer or an architect, who can then provide further insight into the available options. The next step is for the designer or architect to present a customized plan and work directly with a contractor to explain the design and spatial requirements to achieve the client's vision. The use of drawings and planning is often required to identify the correct technical aspects and architectural possibilities. In certain circumstances, building (and building department) approvals may be required, depending on the changes involved.

Small architectural changes can greatly improve the overall function and aesthetics of a home. If executed correctly, these changes can directly increase the value and purchase price of the home should the resident choose to one day sell or rent the space. People buy what they see, and these renovations very much add to the allure of a home. If the client chooses to go down this path, a door to new options and possibilities opens. Small renovations add more flexibility and allow for customized results, which are usually more satisfying and desirable for the client.

However, construction work can be costly and time consuming, as it involves selecting and coordinating with multiple parties, such as contractors, technicians, professional designers and building management companies should you need to obtain permission. A primary deterrent in this area is often the fear of uncertainty. The idea of pursuing permanent changes to a home without exact knowledge of the final cost, time and outcome or how to get started may be intimidating enough to make you scratch the idea completely — especially if you're pursuing this initiative without professional guidance. Plus, some buildings require pre-approval for such work, and the management company may reject the renovation altogether if the changes are not in line with the overall vision for the property. Meanwhile, some people might be deterred from renovating their homes so as to avoid the inconvenience of conducting work on the apartment while living in the space. All of these factors make it all the more important to select the right team to conduct your work. Many of these concerns and inconveniences can be significantly reduced by working with an experienced and qualified interior designer or architect who can guide you through the process, manage expectations and provide helpful solutions.

Although prices are subject to change and depend on the scope of work as well as professional fees, an average or reasonable price range for small renovations (inclusive of all materials and service fees, such as those for labor and expertise) if you are looking for a significant impact on aesthetics, functionality and investment value is between $10,000 and $50,000 over a one- to two-year period. However, you can choose to spend as little as $1,000 to $5,000 should you implement only a few of these techniques.

Again, the above price range is subjective, as it depends on the number of changes and the complexity of the work that the client desires.

There are three primary costs associated with this type of work: fees for professional design (by a designer or architect), labor costs (costs associated with the work conducted by the contractor who builds the space as instructed by the professional) and cost of materials used to build the space (e.g., drywall, lights, cabinetry, paint, etc.). For smaller construction projects such as those noted here, an architect may charge fees (in addition to those for labor and materials costs) that range from 20 to 25 percent of the construction cost. So, if a project costs $10,000 in labor and materials, an architect might charge approximately $2,500 for his services.

For best results and to manage the risk of damage on larger-scale architectural changes, consider working with a designer or architect instead of working directly with the contractor. For less complex enhancements, such as those relating to installations for minor surface changes, consider working with a designer.

The price information provided herein is for reference purposes only and is based on New York City estimates. Although the author has made every attempt to provide price information that is representative, the prices noted below are intended to reflect the author's viewpoint on what is an expected or reasonable cost for which the relevant tip or technique may be addressed while also keeping true to the specific objectives and quality standards expressed in this guide. The actual price will depend on a variety of factors, including the quality of service/materials, location, the current market and the scope of work.

LIGHTING

For those who want a cleaner and more custom lighting scheme that fits with their personal needs (whether they be functional or aesthetic), the option of a small lighting renovation provides new possibilities: better lighting with fewer sources, architectural and artistic interest, convenience through the use of light switches as opposed to multiple methods for turning lights on and off, and additional flexibility and control. Below are some examples of interesting improvements should you choose to pursue this route.

INSTALL DOWNLIGHTS FOR A CLEANER, MORE DISCREET LOOK

Downlights are recessed lights (typically round) that are built directly into hollow openings or spaces within the ceiling. They cast narrow beams of light and differ from overhead fixtures in that they are often smaller and embedded within the ceiling or a similar surface, such as within the top of a niche or cabinet. As these types of lights do not protrude and are somewhat hidden, they provide a cleaner, more discreet look while also taking up less space. The advantage of using downlights as opposed to other lighting schemes is that this type of lighting reaches spaces that are generally smaller, darker and harder to illuminate, such as corners and counters.

These lights can be used for general ambient lighting based on how many are installed and where they are located. Depending on the size of the downlight and the bulb, a single downlight can cast as much as 150 watts of light into a room. For ceilings that are too low to accommodate an overhead fixture (something common in smaller spaces), downlights can be instrumental. Downlights can also be used for focused task lighting if they are placed directly over a specific wall or object. For example, downlights placed strategically in niches can accentuate both an object and the wall into which it is placed, thus creating a decorative enhancement. A more functional application is to install a small downlight in a closet or within cabinetry to illuminate a specific area and improve visibility without much disruption to the space.

Although subject to change, an average or reasonable price range for installing downlights into a Sheetrock surface (materials and service costs — excluding interior design or architect fees) may be between

$250 and $1,500. The cost to purchase and install a single downlight is approximately $250 (including the cost for the labor/installation). If you are looking to install a series of six (which is a common number when dealing with downlights) throughout the ceiling, the cost would be closer to $1,500 for the lights and labor installation. In instances in which downlights are being installed into non-Sheetrock surfaces that are harder and require more labor for the electrician or contractor, the cost will be around $150 more per downlight.

INSTALL SCONCES FOR DECORATIVE AMBIENT LIGHTING AND SPACE-SAVING CAPABILITIES

Sconces are highly decorative light fixtures that are affixed directly onto the wall with no base or other apparent form of support. They come in a variety of materials and finishes and provide powerful multidirectional ambient lighting. In addition, they serve as a great solution for those who don't have electrical capabilities in the ceiling.

Sconces are best installed at a height where the light bulb is located approximately 66 inches above the floor. To ensure the brightest lighting, it is best to find a high-wattage sconce made of clear or white glass and set on a dimmer. Generally LED sconces provide the most benefits, as LED lighting is not only cost effective but also provides better-quality light than fluorescent or incandescent lighting. Nowadays you can put LED or halogen bulbs in most sconces and fixtures.

Sconces provide powerful lighting and free up space. Sconces offer a multitude of benefits in smaller spaces. In addition to creating aesthetic appeal and elegance (in contrast to downlights, which are designed to be hidden and covert), sconces supply powerful lighting and save valuable floor space. That makes them an extremely attractive substitute for floor lamps and other pieces that rest on the floor and have inconvenient, messy wires. If the sconce is installed with a light switch or similar switching capability, you have the ability to designate a convenient location of your preference for controlling the light. You can enhance the design of a space by selecting interesting and intriguing sconces or by positioning them in creative ways. For instance, two sconces can be placed on either side of a fireplace, a piece of artwork or a mirror to add balance and proportion to a room as well as provide the room with excellent lighting. Meanwhile, sconces can be valuable light sources. Adding a sconce over the top of a door, for example, is a good solution for creating an entry light in an area that usually doesn't get much light in the first place. This type of lighting also works beautifully in hallways, where overhead lighting might not exist.

Sconces can define space and serve as exceptional focal points. Sconces can be used to visually highlight a space and discreetly distinguish a separate area of the apartment without building a wall. For example, if you want to create an interesting foyer, you could assemble an attractive vignette by positioning a picture or mirror between a set of sconces and placing a table below. This setup would define the area and create a focal point due to the lighting from the sconces, which would accentuate the furniture and accessories while creating a boundary between the neighboring spaces. This arrangement can be achieved without the use of sconces, too, but the sconces work to further define the space through the creative application of light, which centers and groups the pieces together.

Sconces require installation work. Sconces generally require low-intensity installation work because many buildings do not provide electrical wiring within the general region where you would want to install a sconce (e.g., on the center of the wall). In order to accommodate that, enlist the help of an electrician to pull electricity from other nearby electrical sources (such as those within the baseboard near the floor). This method involves physically rerouting the wires (or adding wires from the original source) and pulling them through the wall to the desired location, where the electrician can then drill a hole and create an outlet. All of this work happens behind the wall and is hidden from view.

Although subject to change, an average or reasonable price range for work involving a pair of sconces (materials and service costs — excluding interior design or architect fees) may be between $400 and $1,500. This amount includes the cost of purchasing two sconces and installation work. Sconce prices vary depending on how many you want and also on the particular sconce you select; however, you can obtain an attractive sconce for between $150 and $750. Installation, which generally ranges from $100 to $200 depending on the complexity of the work, involves running wires from an electrical source to the location of the sconce as *well as painting and patching any subsequent holes in the wall that may result from the work performed.*

CONSIDER CREATIVE APPLICATIONS FOR NON-FIXTURE STRIP LED LIGHTING

Non-fixture strip LED bulbs are a series of several small bulbs that are mounted together in a row through a bendable wire, string or tube. Because they are all linked together without the restriction of a fixture, they are very flexible in terms of placement. Due to the size and number of bulbs, this type of lighting scheme tends to last an extremely long time and does not generate much heat, and thus has a longer life than regular bulbs.

By creatively placing small strip lights on flying beams, bookcases, cabinetry or partial walls, you can have an additional lighting source that is discreet and cost effective (since strip bulbs are easy to install and inexpensive). Because of their size and flexibility, strip bulbs provide conveniences such as lighting up the ceiling or hard-to-reach locations, like beneath a cabinet or ledge. Particularly bright lighting may be obtained by using multiple LED bulbs. At lower outputs, these lights provide great mood lighting, similar to cove lighting (a form of indirect lighting built into ledges, recesses or valances in a ceiling). Although strip bulbs can be used for a variety of purposes, an imaginative application is for aesthetic accent lighting, especially to highlight decorative ceilings and provide a warm and even-lit lighting scheme. As an added benefit, they can be connected to a dimmer for additional control over the level of light output.

Although subject to change, an average or reasonable price range for work involving non-fixture strip LED lighting (materials and service costs — excluding interior design or architect fees) may be between $700 and $900.

KEY BENEFITS OF A LIGHTING RENOVATION

- Cleaner and more custom lighting schemes that offer additional architectural and artistic interest, convenience and impact.

- Downlights, which can be installed with only a small renovation (unless installed within a cabinet), provide a sleek, discreet and flexible lighting option with a sophisticated look. They offer powerful ambient and task lighting, take up less room and reach additional areas that cannot be accessed by traditional light fixtures.

- Sconces, another lighting source that requires installation, serve as a highly decorative and aesthetic option for strong ambient lighting. They save space by attaching onto a wall and offer convenience through the flexibility of a light switch, which allows you to avoid messy wires. They can be positioned within a space to creatively add balance, proportion and boundaries.

- Strip lights provide inexpensive placement options that have a long life span. They serve as an additional and discreet light source for mood lighting.

ARCHITECTURAL CHANGES

The beauty of working with a professional architect or designer to implement architectural changes is that you essentially have the power to manipulate your space to your liking in ways that you never thought possible, whether it be adding doors, changing the floor, creating walls, altering the ceiling height, combining rooms or building additional storage space. However, the current layout of your space will influence what you can and cannot do, so it helps to confer with a professional to better understand your options.

REINVENT YOUR FLOOR WITH TILES

Contrary to what many may think, floors can be completely altered or redesigned at a reasonable cost, which is one of the more notable benefits of smaller spaces. If you are looking to do something interesting with the floor other than using carpeting or rugs, you can experiment with tiles or stone flooring, to name a couple of options.

Enhancing the Floor With Tiles

To accentuate the floors and introduce a new artistic element, you can create a completely new floor with a unique design by using tiles. The kitchen, bathroom and foyer area are all ideal areas for tile floors. Stone or ceramic/porcelain tiles work great in each of those areas, as the tiles are durable, smooth and easy to clean. You can use tile throughout the apartment if you are going for a more modern and chic feel; however, this will be more expensive. Porcelain tends to be less expensive than stones like marble, granite or limestone. You can find reasonably priced porcelain or stone tiles at stores such as New York City's Nemo Tile, or you can find more expensive, high-end tiles at stores such as New York City's Artistic Tile or Ann Sacks. When choosing tiles, it is important to select patterns that are similar in design and feel to the rest of the apartment since too many differences within a small space will make the area look smaller than it already is.

General Tile Tips

In addition to offering cosmetic enhancement and ease of cleaning, tile floors can make a room appear larger when the tiles are positioned on a diagonal. This is because it is easier for the eye to follow the lines on the tiles as they move continuously outward, thus creating the illusion of a larger and ever-broadening space. The added benefit of placing tiles on a diagonal is that you can avoid fussing with the grout lines in an effort to make sure that the lines align with the walls, cabinets or other objects positioned on the floor and wall above. Grout lines are the white, sandy cement filler material that you see between tiles. They work to fill the void and connect the tiles to one another. From a design perspective, if you place tiles parallel to the walls (in contrast to the diagonal approach), you are really taking on the exercise of ensuring that the grout lines of the tiles are visually aligned with the walls, cabinets or other objects. As you can imagine, this is a time-intensive activity that might not have a strong outcome. Although additional tiles are needed in order to design the floor on a diagonal, the difference in cost is minimal, and the result is substantial.

When working with tile floors, it is important to ensure that the individual tiles are placed closely together. This will de-emphasize the grout lines, which tend to discolor after time (especially in high-traffic areas), thus creating the potential for an uneven and dirty look. Unfortunately, contractors may have an incentive to use larger grout lines so as to avoid the additional effort of lining up the pieces so that they are precise. This is why you should be sure to specifically indicate that you prefer to have the tiles positioned closely to one another.

Although subject to change, an average or reasonable price range for installing tile floors (materials and service costs — excluding interior design or architect fees) may be between $750 and $1,200 for one small space (such as a foyer, bathroom or kitchen) and between $1,400 and $2,200 for two small spaces. The labor costs decrease exponentially as you apply tiles to additional spaces since the work can be performed simultaneously and existing resources can be leveraged. Therefore, if you are planning to lay tiles in more than one area, it pays to perform the work at the same time.

LOWER THE CEILING HEIGHT TO ENLARGE THE SPACE AND ACHIEVE BETTER BALANCE

Here's a useful visual effect that most wouldn't think to take advantage of: If a smaller room's ceiling height is lower than an adjacent larger room's ceiling height (such as a hallway leading to a living room or a small entry leading to a larger room), then the larger room's ceiling will feel much higher. Even lowering the smaller room's ceiling by just a few inches will make the larger room's ceiling feel appreciably higher. This technique is particularly helpful for narrow spaces. For example, dropping the ceiling in a narrow hallway, if only slightly, will make the side walls feel more expansive, thus negating the tunnel effect while balancing the overall proportion of the space.

Physically lowering the ceiling (or a piece of the ceiling) involves using a contractor to add a new Sheetrock ceiling below the existing ceiling. This construction project is relatively painless and provides ongoing benefits relative to the cost. If the thought of physically altering the ceiling frightens you, or if you are looking for an alternative solution, a similar impact can be achieved by painting the ceiling a darker color or a darker shade of the wall color. This will create the illusion of a lower ceiling. See Change Proportions Through Visually Manipulating Ceiling Height for further discussion on using paint to expand space.

Although subject to change, an average or reasonable price range for lowering the ceiling in a smaller space, such as a hallway or small room (materials and service costs — excluding interior design or architect fees) may be between $1,500 and $3,500, where the lower price might be for a 5-foot-by-4-foot hallway ceiling and the upper range for a 10-foot-by-12-foot ceiling.

BUILD PARTIAL WALLS OR CABINETRY PARTITIONS TO ENLARGE THE SPACE

A partial wall is exactly what it sounds like: a normal wall that rises up from the floor and extends toward the ceiling, but it never directly connects with the ceiling. Thus it is essentially a strongly rooted partition with an opening between the top of the wall and the ceiling. The beauty of this type of wall is that it can take on any height depending on how you would like to use it. Common heights are:

- 30 to 36 inches from the floor (or a *knee wall*), so the top of the wall is approximately countertop height or the height of an average restaurant bar.

- 72 to 84 inches from the floor (or a *three-fourths wall*), so the top of the wall is approximately the height of a bookcase or door screen.

- 3 to 12 inches from the ceiling (or a *seven-eighths wall*), so the top of the wall is approximately the height of the ceiling, with only a small space serving as a gap.

A partial wall is commonly covered with Sheetrock but can also be built using sturdier materials (for a higher cost), such as a piece of cabinetry (usually made of wood). The wall may be curved, straight, tall or short and can be constructed in any number of configurations. Plus, the ability to play with the wall's architectural features sets the stage for many artistic and decorative alterations. In apartments or lofts where a more open and airy feeling is desired, a partial wall inherits a sleek, floating and sculptural presence and is an extraordinarily successful solution for not feeling cramped.

One other interesting feature is that the wall can serve as a separation device between two or more spaces without presenting itself as an obstruction. The reason for this is due to how the human eye perceives space and places visual emphasis on what exists at eye level. Depending on the height of a partial wall and how it relates to the overall space, it can naturally blend in with a person's peripheral vision rather than be perceived as an enclosure or interruption. In other words, the wall is less intrusive and allows the room to feel open.

Half or three-fourths walls introduce definition of space through the use of barriers that maintain circulation and flow. This is particularly effective in the kitchen: You can instantly and remarkably enlarge the entire apartment by opening the kitchen so it flows into the rest of the apartment. This can be accomplished by tearing down part of an intervening wall (leaving an open space between the ceiling and the top of the wall) or by puncturing an opening between upper and lower cabinets (this works if there is a wall in the kitchen that is made of cabinetry and not too difficult to tear down). Also, if the wall between the kitchen and breakfast area is removed or replaced with a partial wall, the entire space will appear expansive yet distinct. With a loft-like kitchen, the overall apartment is still defined but feels more spacious.

In addition, cabinetry made of wood or similar material can be used as a partial wall in place of a Sheetrock wall. Like partial walls, cabinetry can mediate between rooms, eliminating the need for a full wall with the added benefit of providing storage. Cabinetry can be designed as bookcases, drawer units or even tables dividing different areas of a room. For example, in the dining room, counter-height cabinetry can be built to serve as a piece of furniture that mediates between the kitchen and dining areas while simultaneously acting as storage space for dishes and cutlery on one side and perhaps as a stereo enclosure on the other. Or you could build a counter-height bookcase that serves as a counter for two adjoining areas of a room; it can be a bookcase on one side and a plain piece of cabinetry supporting a flat-screen TV on the other side.

Although subject to change, an average or reasonable price range for work such as building partial walls or cabinetry partitions (materials and service costs — excluding interior design or architect fees) may be between $1,000 and $3,500, where the lower price relates to a wall that is

*smaller, simpler or made primarily of Sheetrock; the higher range reflects
a wall that is more complex and larger or requires cabinetry.*

INSTALL A GLASS BLOCK OR SANDBLASTED GLASS WALL

To further enhance the intrigue and sophistication of a room
while artistically defining the space, you can create a full or partial wall using glass blocks or sandblasted glass. These types of
walls get an A+ for small apartment use, as they create a sense of
closure and separation of space in a light, bright and airy manner.

A glass block wall refers to a wall made of glass bricks that
you can see through but not completely, as the wall is constructed
to be translucent but not transparent. Like regular walls, glass
block walls are thick and substantial and can stand alone from
floor to ceiling. Glass blocks come in a variety of different shapes,
sizes and colors.

Sandblasted glass refers primarily to a sheet of glass that has
been sanded to feel coarse and translucent and placed within a

wall structure. Sandblasted glass is more commonly used because it lends itself to a modern or traditional style, whereas glass block walls tend to be more suitable for a modern look only.

A glass wall is a particularly interesting design application that provides a subtle barrier while simultaneously allowing for the free passage of light. This means a glass block wall can brighten areas that don't have windows or might not ordinarily have access to light. Because glass block walls have a rippled surface and sandblasted glass is not completely transparent, the image you see through a wall crafted from either material is muted, which provides for more privacy, among other purposes.

Whether you decide to build a wall completely out of glass or with partial glass (i.e., embed a portion of glass within a Sheetrock wall), a glass wall is a small construction job that requires a contractor. It can be completed in three to five days. Should glass blocks prove too costly, an alternative could be to build a Sheetrock wall at counter-height level and then install a sheet of sandblasted glass, similar to a window, which can be built up to (but not necessarily touching) the ceiling. This arrangement will allow for both the stability of a wall and the translucency of glass. Note that partial walls need to be anchored and stabilized as appropriate.

Although subject to change, an average or reasonable price range for work involving glass block or sandblasted glass walls (materials and service costs — excluding interior design or architect fees) may be between $1,000 and $2,500 for a glass block wall and between $750 and $1,500 for a sandblasted glass wall (not including the surrounding Sheetrock wall). Sandblasted glass tends to be less expensive because it's a single sheet of glass, whereas with glass blocks, you are also paying for special assembly, which includes a method for keeping all the blocks together.

CREATE A NICHE

A niche is a shallow, carved-out indentation within a wall or piece of cabinetry. Niches can be almost any shape: round, square, rectangular. They can also be adorned with detailed plasterwork moldings or carvings to further accentuate their allure.

Niches provide both functional and aesthetic interior design features. Function-wise, one of the biggest benefits is the advantage of a ledge, which can be used to display a variety of objects, such as vases, sculptures or art. A creative application is to place a sheet of glass or wood on the ledge for both protection of the surface below and for decorative interest. From a design standpoint, niches can make spaces look larger and more interesting by creating a sense of something existing beyond. They add a magical feel of depth to a space — one that can be further enhanced by installing mirrors on the back of the niche (if the niche is flat). Because niches are sometimes constructed at counter height or above and offer a natural touch of architectural interest, they can serve as convenient focal points, as well.

Niches also provide the flexibility and foundation for further enhancements in the sense that they are particularly customizable. For example, you can use the hollow space beneath the niche as storage (by building or installing cabinetry).

Although subject to change, an average or reasonable price range for work involving niches that are approximately 3 feet by 6 feet (materials and service costs — excluding interior design or architect fees) may be between $1,000 and $1,500.

CREATE A RECESSED WALL

Recessed walls are similar to niches except they are larger and tend to take up a greater portion of the wall surface. If it's hard to visualize what a recessed wall looks like, imagine that your apartment wall is made of malleable putty. Now pretend that you take your hand and apply enough pressure to indent the wall everywhere except for about a foot from the top of the wall, across the whole wall. This would essentially create two walls: a recessed "back" wall (the wall that was created from the indentation) and a "front" wall (the narrow area that is about a foot from the top of the wall). A recessed wall can take on many shapes and sizes, just like a niche.

Recessed walls are often created by having a contractor add plaster or Sheetrock on top of an existing wall to create somewhat of an outer layer, thus resulting in two parallel but different walls. Although building a recessed wall actually consists of adding more wall (e.g., the plaster or Sheetrock that forms the front wall), this enhancement establishes a visual illusion that looks like the back wall has been pushed back, adding depth to a space while simultaneously introducing enhanced definition. If you paint the back and front walls the same color — even if the back wall is only 3 inches deeper — it will appear as though the back wall is significantly deeper and painted with a darker color, thereby adding the appearance of color and tonal variation.

Although subject to change, an average or reasonable price range for work relating to a recessed wall that is approximately 8 feet by 4 feet wide and 6 inches deep (materials and service costs — excluding interior design or architect fees) may be between $600 and $1,000.

DON'T RESTRICT YOURSELF TO ONE TYPE OF DOOR: THINK OUTSIDE OF THE FRAME

The concept of a door is pretty straightforward, but most people don't think to change things up by considering different door types or schemes. Doors can slide, glide or hide. Whatever your preference, it is worth exploring some of the more creative door options. By thinking beyond the traditional door, you can attain a cleaner, larger and better-functioning space.

Pocket (Sliding) Doors

Pocket doors are perfect for small spaces because they conveniently open and close by sliding in and out of a wall. This lightweight option doesn't take up the space of a traditional swinging door and is a great solution for tight spaces where a traditional door that swivels open and closed may become burdensome or create undesired contact with nearby walls or other constructs. In fact, pocket doors can save an average of 10 square feet of floor space. Meanwhile, pocket doors also function as moveable walls that can be hinged, tracked or concealed, and they pose no barriers when stored in the wall. In addition, they can look more interesting if they are assembled with unique materials, such as attractive hardware for pulling the doors open.

Although subject to change, an average or reasonable price range for work involving one pocket door and one new wall to accommodate the *door (materials and service costs — excluding interior design or architect fees) may be between $2,500 and $3,000. This cost includes all related hardware as well as the cost of replacing a regular hinged door with a sliding door, which would involve adding another wall (one wall in front of the existing wall) to create a pocket for the door to slide into.*

Barn Doors

Similar to pocket doors, barn doors are full-sized doors that slide open and closed; however, the key difference is that barn doors slide over the wall as opposed to into the wall. When the door is closed, the door and the wall form a flat, smooth surface. When the door slides over the Sheetrock next to it, it creates a double-wall-like effect. Barn doors are deceiving in their simplicity; it can be difficult to build this kind of door correctly because the wall or floor stops (the objects that prevent the door from sliding past where it is supposed to) have to be designed to ensure full closure when extended and perfect alignment when positioned over the Sheetrock wall.

There are many clever and useful applications for barn doors. Like the pocket door, there is room to embellish and decorate each side of the door. An interesting application would be to apply a mirror to one or both sides, so that when standing in front of or behind the door, the space appears mystically enlarged. You can also build a portion of the barn doors with glass so that when the barn door is closed, the room gets additional light from the surrounding areas.

Although subject to change, an average or reasonable price range for one full-sized barn door (materials and service costs — excluding interior design or architect fees) such as this may be between $600 and $1,000. This includes installation of the track mechanism and all related hardware that allows the door to slide.

Blind Doors

Blind doors (also called *concealed* or *false doors*) are discreet in that they do not appear to be doors — they simply blend in with the wall. This is because they can be constructed without the use of blatant frames, hardware or traditional door structures. For instance, blind doors can be built with edge pulls that allow the door to pivot open when you push the door, or you can add subtle knobs or handles to move the door as desired. Overall, hardware is usually concealed, both at the top of the door and at the bottom of the door frame. If you are looking to create incognito storage spaces or cabinetry or want a cleaner wall palette, blind doors are a phenomenal option. These doors are particularly useful in smaller spaces where it is important to have a crisp look.

Although subject to change, an average or reasonable price range for one full-sized blind door (materials and service costs — excluding interior design or architect fees) may be between $750 and $1,200. This price includes all related hardware that allows the door to open and close.

BUILT-IN CABINETRY

If there is one architectural enhancement that will provide instant value without any drawbacks, it's built-in cabinetry. You can point to just about any part of your apartment that you find unattractive or that you feel is off and immediately enrich it with the clever use of cabinetry. Built-in cabinetry is extremely cost effective and flexible and provides functional and aesthetic advantages in a short amount of time. By using built-in cabinetry, you can implement just about any feature that a freestanding piece of furniture can incorporate. Designed correctly, this type of cabinetry provides additional storage and offers an inconspicuous presence.

Any piece of furniture that is attached to a wall (and thus "fixed") is ostensibly considered to be built-in. For example, modern kitchen cabinets that are proportioned and designed to fit within two specific walls (e.g., under a soffit and covered with a custom-sized stone top) are considered built-ins. Built-in cabinetry offers a variety of options, such as doors, drawers, tops or bottoms, and can take the shape of a bench, window seat, dining buffet, bookcase, bed, media center and so forth. The cabinetry can be made of plywood or a variety of less expensive compressed woods, such as medium-density fiberboard. For a fancier look, you can use more refined and finished woods, such as mahogany. These types of pieces can also display moldings, glass or ornamental plasterwork. You can choose one piece of cabinetry or a series depending on your budget and preferences.

Cabinets are generally quiet pieces of furniture in the sense that they are subtle additions that perform valuable functions. From an interior design perspective, they offer elegance and intrigue, as they are custom-sized to fit a particular area and provide a sleek appearance. In addition, if you choose to install cabinetry that spans from one side of a room to the other, you can effectively influence the entire appearance of the room by creating a better balance and smoothing out any asymmetries that exist.

Another way cabinetry enhances smaller spaces is by disguising less attractive fixed parts of the apartment such as an air conditioner or radiator. For instance, instead of just covering the radiator with an unattractive cover, you can custom-build cabinetry over the radiator to camouflage the appearance and attain both cosmetic advantages and additional storage options. Note that cabinetry built over a radiator or an air conditioner will need to allow for proper air circulation.

Although subject to change, an average or reasonable price range for work involving built-in cabinetry (materials and service costs — excluding interior design or architect fees) may be between $500 and $5,000.

The lower price range relates to more simple cabinetry work, such as a 3-foot-by-3-foot prefabricated radiator cover made of composite board. The higher end of the range relates to larger and more complex projects, such as an 8-foot-by-3-foot unit made of wood veneer. Cabinetry made of wood will be more expensive than composite board. For prices relating to even larger and more complex cabinetry projects involving walls, see Build Partial Walls or Cabinetry Partitions to Enlarge the Space.

KEY BENEFITS OF IMPLEMENTING ARCHITECTURAL CHANGES

- Allows you to manipulate the space to your liking, such as by changing the floor, creating walls, altering the ceiling height, combining rooms, adding doors and building additional storage space.

- Provides an instant and dramatic enhancement to the decor and aesthetics of the apartment.

- Offers durable, permanent and long-lasting improvements that increase the value of the space.

- Physically enhances the space to achieve an overall stronger layout with improved functionality and circulation.

Additional Tricks of the Trade!

Do-It-Yourself (Without a Designer)

Create Your Own Art

One clever and inexpensive way of introducing a unique and decorative flavor into your space is to create your own artwork. That doesn't mean that you have to be an artist or start from scratch.

Rather, this option involves creatively experimenting with what you already have to come up with something interesting. You can start by taking a scarf or a piece of fabric that you think has a strong artistic element, such as a fascinating pattern. Next, frame it. The frame can be a simple, thin metal frame (black, chrome, gold or brass should all be fine). Alternatively, you can highlight the fabric even more by purchasing a frameless Plexiglas picture cover. When creating your own art, it is important that the wall is an appropriate background for the item. For instance, a white wall works best with colorful scarves. For a more monochromatic scarf, a vivid-colored wall works best. If you have a series of smaller scarves (or equivalent fabrics), you can play with grouping them along the wall to create one nice visual image.

Select Accessories That Can Be Affixed to the Walls

Common items such as mirrors, shelves, desks and ledges can all be affixed to a wall and save valuable space. In bedrooms, for example, it is helpful to attach a clock to a wall as opposed to setting it on a desk. Decorative wood ledges can be easily affixed to a wall over the night table or on the sides of the bed to provide a convenient space for displaying or storing objects while also offering aesthetic value. This strategy is particularly helpful near the entrance of the apartment. As we all know, things you carry into your apartment that don't have a home — like the mail or magazines and newspapers — will most likely end up on the floor or the first available spot, sitting around as clutter for days to come. For this reason, it is important to have designated spaces for your belongings, especially for when you first walk through the door. Easy and convenient options such as shelves or a few hooks for your coat, keys or bags will go a long way. Have a look around the entrance area and think of some simple, creative solutions, like installing a small ledge or putting up a nice series of hooks. You will be surprised by the big impact these small adjustments provide.

Use Wall-Hung Floating Shelves

The key feature of floating shelves is that the hardware is hidden behind the shelf, thus delivering a clean and neat floating appearance, as if the shelves are glued to the Sheetrock or plaster. These shelves are a wonderful solution for providing storage space for smaller items or displaying decorations. For example, a small floating shelf may function as entry hall furniture (like a ledge upon which to put your keys) or as a serving counter in the dining room (if wide enough). They can also work as interesting focal points if hung at eye level, as they can be used for displaying numerous things such as artwork, personal collections or anything that's not too wide. Here's how to determine how high to hang the shelf: Look at what else is hanging on your walls (pictures and so forth), and hang the shelf at that same height to establish visual consistency by creating an invisible line throughout the room (sometimes referred to as a *datum line*).

Pay Attention to Detail

Small details allow you to highlight an apartment's strong features and deflect attention from less appealing areas. A mirror with a unique finish, a wall with a special treatment or a kitchen backsplash with interesting tiles can all have a vast impact. Or this can be as simple as selecting intriguing hardware or other accessories, such as cabinet knobs or locks. Changing the kitchen cabinet knobs, for instance, usually dramatically increases the attractiveness of the kitchen. Contrary to what one may think, small enhancements are arguably more noticeable in a smaller space; in a larger space, details can become lost.

Avoid Track Lighting Where Possible Unless Purely Aesthetic

Track lighting is effective for focused lighting, such as for targeting a painting or a piece of wall, but it is not so helpful for general ambient lighting. It is a common misconception that track lights provide more light. In reality, track lighting is often more limited in reach, and oftentimes the bulbs on a track are glaring.

Paint Cabinetry and Moldings the Same Color as the Wall

Painting built-in cabinetry (excluding fine wood or metal cabinets) and molding is an effective way to use color to enhance the overall interest and appeal of the apartment. The trick here is to paint the cabinets and molding the same color as the wall upon which they are affixed. For cabinetry, this technique will allow the pieces to blend in and become recessive, thus making your space feel larger. (Note that for moldings and cabinetry made of wood, a slightly higher gloss finish level is necessary because wood needs a glossy paint finish, so even if the moldings or cabinetry have the same paint color as the wall, the finish level will create the appearance of a different shade of that color — and that's just fine.) On occasion, if a piece is distinct and unique, painting it a slightly different color from the walls can accentuate the piece and look quite stunning; however, this will work only if the selected color variation and tone is subtle. Moldings tend to cut up wall surfaces, so unless the surface is quite large and the molding is in excellent condition, it works best to direct the focus away from moldings. In large homes, painting moldings a contrast color is quite common, and it is usually effective because the breadth of the room can handle it. However, in small spaces, such a distinction will visually chop up the surface and should be avoided so as to divert a discontinuity within the space.

Use Fewer and Higher-Quality Items

It may seem like a no-brainer that when you have less space, you should have less stuff. Not as much thought, however, is given to the importance of investing in higher-quality items — mainly because people just don't feel that it is worth the research time or the money. But investing in high-quality items doesn't have to equal spending tons of money. It does, however, mean that you should avoid poorly made pieces that look cheap and don't fit with the theme of the apartment. This is especially important for multifunctional pieces that are of poor quality and have short life spans. By using high-quality but simple pieces of furniture, fabrics, finishes or accessories, you can create an elegant and consistent appearance in your home. For example, poorer-quality wood that is too grainy appears cheap. Cheap woods include pressboard, unfinished plywood and synthetic laminates that are made to look like wood. You can easily spot unattractive grain patterns by looking for wood that reflects a choppy stain that appears uneven on the surface. In addition, many of these woods lose their initial attractiveness after a short period of time and you begin to see more grain and roughness. They also have the tendency to fade if near sunlight. Instead, you want to choose a smooth-looking wood with tight graining and not too much texture.

Use Textures and Finishes That Are Sleek, Simple and Elegant

Tone-on-tone patterns, such as blue on blue (same color), in two different fabric weaves (such as cotton and velvet) offer variation yet are visually similar and do not create an optical distraction. These types of patterns tend to be simple yet powerful, thus creating a subtle diversity. Finishes should be quieter and have different tonal values that are similar, such as darker or lighter shades of the same color. Quiet, neutral colors and finishes that are not too grainy or textured are best because they complement other furnishings rather than compete with them. For fabrics, it's good to use active, bold patterns with bright colors and large-size prints and patterns as accent pieces rather than as main items. For example, if you have a white or beige couch and want to add color and pattern, try using a decorative pillow that is a solid, bold color like lime green or orange, with or without a large floral or geometric pattern. However, keep the diversity of patterns to a minimum. Too many patterns in one space is distracting and troubling to the eye. Refined means good quality, and quiet means not too many competing patterns.

Use Durable Finishes

Good things tend to age gracefully. Better materials look better, wear better and last longer, so it is best to use natural substances that persevere and look good over time. Stone generally doesn't chip like ceramic tiles, and cheap woods discolor more easily since they don't have protective coats and tend to soak up environmental elements, such as sunlight. Cheap fabrics and paint also don't wear well over time. Other materials to avoid include plastic laminates, metals that are not solid or brass coated and thinly veneered leathers that are not scratch-resistant. Plumbing fittings (such as faucets and knobs) should have protective finishes (try chrome) so that they don't turn dull, brown or pitted. Nondurable finishes negatively affect a space by making the space look old and tired before its time. Spending a little more where it counts goes a long way and reduces costs in the long run.

With a Designer
Experiment With the Floors Through Staining Wood

If you have wooden floors (and almost all floors are wooden at the core) and you would like to emphasize the furniture and overall grandeur of a room, you can stain the entire floor a very dark brown or black. This will have the effect of shifting the focus onto the furniture and accentuating other objects that may rest on top of the floor. Staining the floor works well in instances in which you have nice furniture or where the floors are uneven or lack appeal. By directing the focus off the floor, you can also reduce the noise within the room, which will make the space appear larger and cleaner.

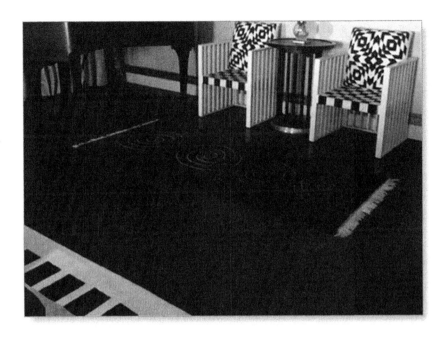

Use Wainscoting to Define Barriers and Achieve Comfortable Living

Bigger and taller is not always better. Small children and pets love small and cozy spaces. The confines of a crib are comforting to babies. Pets know how good it feels to nestle up to a corner or a wall. In fact, people in general prefer close points of reference and contact. Most people instinctively choose to sit in the corners of sofas as opposed to the middle. Why? Because large rooms can make a person feel uncomfortable or even lost and overwhelmed by the open space. Humanist architects addressed this issue through wainscoting, a trick for making an inhabitant feel more comfortable in a large or high-ceilinged room.

Wainscoting is a technique that generally involves wooden paneling lining the lower parts of a wall (usually spanning from the top of the baseboard of the wall to around chair-rail height or close to the top of most furniture, approximately 24 to 36 inches from the floor). Although wainscoting typically involves wood, its effect can be simulated by using fabric or other material. Even in a modern setting, wainscoting can break up a wall mass and allow the eye to rest at a level more suitable for human proportions. A useful tip that can be applied to your bedroom is to position the wainscoting so that the top of the chair-rail lines up with the top of the mattress and bedding, creating one consistent datum line throughout. When a person lies in bed, the surrounding chair-rail and wainscoting will help a person feel enclosed. Wrapping a space with wood or a soft layer of fabric tends to have the effect of making you feel warm and safe, often resulting in better overall sleep. The same guidelines apply to the living room and dining room: Wainscoting should be applied from the baseboard of the wall up to or around chair-rail height or the top of the furniture. In the dining room, for example, wainscoting should be aligned with the top of a table, at approximately 30 inches high.

Use Recessive Built-In Mirrors to Expand Space and Reflect Light

Recessive mirrors (also called *blind mirrors*) are architectural mirrors that are relatively discreet and often have no frame or a slim stainless steel or aluminum frame that is barely noticeable. As such, it is often difficult to view them as concrete objects as they tend to recess or disappear into the wall. In general, recessive mirrors are most effective when they are built into cabinetry, a niche or other existing units. By placing recessive mirrors in interesting and obscure locations, these mirrors can covertly expand the surrounding space by capturing and reflecting light. This same effect may be achieved by placing a recessive mirror on a wall between a chair-rail and a ceiling molding so the molding appears to frame the mirror. Because it is often challenging to figure out the best location and use of these mirrors, it is helpful to confer with a professional designer who can properly assess the space, select the correct mirror(s) and determine the location that will be most effective. For a recap of benefits associated with mirrors, see Use Mirrors to Enhance Small Spaces.

Small Renovations
Always Begin With a Master Plan

Similar to an effective interior design plan, a master plan for the overall architectural space should illustrate flow, which, as previously mentioned, is essentially the seductive movement of circulation within and throughout a space. As David Estreich of David Estreich Architects suggests, "The plan dictates a well-fitting relationship between rooms, incorporating a seamless integration of architecture and decoration." Walking through a home should feel right. It should be an elegant movement that glides one through each room, taking in the grace of a space. It's not only the size or style that matters but also the overall composition and how the rooms interplay with one another.

Position Wooden Planks or Carpeting Perpendicular to the Length of the Room

If a room is long and narrow and the floor is made of wooden planks that can be repositioned without too much complication, then the planks should be laid perpendicular to the length of the room (as opposed to parallel). This visually increases the room's breadth and creates better proportions as opposed to making the room look and feel longer than it is. This is also true for carpeting that has a linear striped pattern. Always position this type of carpeting against the grain of the room. If the room is longer in one direction, position the stripe in the opposite direction.

Reveals

Reveals are subtle grooves that are commonly carved into door frames, walls and cabinetry to visually separate two or more architectural elements (such as a door from the frame, or one piece of wood from another). In effect, they provide the appearance of a void between objects and offer an overall lighter feel. From a design perspective, they are essentially add-on luxury enhancements that provide a sophisticated and sleek appearance. The depth of a reveal can be as insignificant as ¼ inch or as deep as several inches. When positioned between the floor and a wall, reveals visually lift the wall off the floor, giving the wall an elevated look. Similarly, a reveal formed by carving out part of a baseboard can enhance the woodwork to provide a lighter, more sculpted look. When situated at the top of a wall, a reveal creates the illusion that the wall is disconnected from the ceiling and somewhat floating.

Create and Define an Entry Foyer Space

The foyer, the initial entry point of the home, is perhaps the most overlooked yet important space. This oftentimes-ignored area is usually nonexistent or underdeveloped unless there is a concerted effort to define it. The entry area of the apartment sets the tone and feel for the entire residence, as it is the first and last impression upon entering and leaving the home. It is here where one is made to feel either welcomed or disoriented. In order to properly define or create this special area, the use of an architect or designer is usually required to carve out additional space from adjoining areas, such as a closet, an existing gallery or a nondescript assigned area. In addition, ceilings can be dropped or raised or both (with the assistance of a contractor). Cove or decorative lighting can be installed, giving the foyer a special aura. Walls can be moved and shaped to create circular, cubed or differently configured spaces. Niches can be added to enhance the foyer's particular aspects. Creative floor patterns can be used to define the area, whether through the elegance of a black-and-white marble floor or the warmth of intricately inlaid woods. Or to give the foyer a fancy appearance, thickly applied Venetian plaster may be added to the walls, and works of art can be placed and highlighted. In addition, the use of glass blocks or sandblasted glass can be employed here and will look especially inviting, as it allows for light to penetrate the space while suggesting what exists beyond. This is one area in which almost any investment will dramatically pay off.

Trade Descriptions

DECORATORS, INTERIOR DESIGNERS, ARCHITECTS AND CONTRACTORS

Interior designers are often asked about the differences between decorators, interior designers and architects. This is a great question. Although there may be overlap and the distinctions can be subtle, each role's unique function can have a radical impact on the intended project.

The most successful projects tend to combine the skills and abilities of decorators, interior designers and architects. Josef Hoffmann, Charles Rennie Mackintosh, Robert Adam, William Morris, Michelangelo, Frank Lloyd Wright and Le Corbusier are among the icons that have excelled in this arena.

It's important to realize that when the designer or decorator places furniture incongruous with the structure, or when the architect designs a space without consideration or respect for how the furnishings will be arranged, the end product is likely to be unsatisfactory. The good news is that design professionals are starting to team up to create comprehensive design alliances to better serve their clients. In essence, the challenge for decorators, interior designers and architects ultimately lies in their ability to seamlessly wed form to function.

So, to begin…

DECORATORS

Decorators embellish and adorn spaces; that is, they are focused on furnishings, interior finishes and existing surfaces. In a way, they add life to a space, creating a three dimensionality that is achieved through its beautification. Typically decorators work with surface decoration such as paint, fabrics, furnishings, decorative lighting and materials. They may also design drapery treatments and specify carpeting, rugs, wallpapers, accessories and soft items. Decorators may not have — or need — a formal design education. While they do deal with tradesmen, such as painters and wallpaper hangers, decorators can often achieve what they need to by being able to create, read or interpret drawings. To this effect, they are not likely to engage in activities involving moving walls, lowering ceilings or adding architectural enhancements to the space. So if your primary need has to do with aesthetics, style and mood, or if you want to refurbish your home but decide that you like the existing plan and feel of the space and have no desire to change the architecture, then the services of a decorator may be sufficient.

INTERIOR DESIGNERS

Interior designers tend to specialize in form, function, space and aesthetics. Although interior designers may decorate, they are professionally trained to create pleasing environments through interior space manipulation and planning. Qualified through education and experience, interior designers identify, research and resolve design issues. They reconfigure interior spaces to make them workable, meeting the specific needs and preferences of the client. Interior designers perform a variety of functions, including:

- Allocating, organizing and arranging a space to suit its function

- Designing lighting schemes (cove lighting, downlights, etc.)

- Monitoring and managing construction or installation work

- Selecting and determining specifications for items such as plumbing fixtures, furnishings and hardware

- Designing color schemes

- Designing and supervising the creation of custom furnishings and details

- Developing documents and specifications related to interior spaces (manuals and schedules delineating the plumbing, finish, hardware, paint and lighting schedules)

- Providing consulting services to help a client determine project goals and objectives

ARCHITECTS

Architects specialize in the molding and manipulation of a space, creating aesthetically pleasing and well-functioning homes, offices or buildings for the client. The major differences between an interior designer and an architect are the architect's education, training, experience and ability to build from the ground up, creating new structures or architectural enhancements. A skilled architect can combine all three skills (decoration, design and architecture), creating a comprehensive work of art.

The residential architect, in particular, can be very masterful in creating a satisfactory built environment, inside and out. "Design architects" can combine great architecture with great design. They are involved with the implementation of a master plan and the outfitting of its interiors. Architects are also knowledgeable about the mechanics of finishes and materials — how and why things work the way they do — and the surrounding environment's relationship to their creation.

CONTRACTORS

Contractors implement the design drawings of the architect or designer. They bring the design professional's vision from a two-dimensional drawing into a three-dimensional reality. As such, they physically build the space and bring to fruition the final design phase. The contractor usually takes direction from the interior designer or architect's aesthetic directives. A skilled contractor will be able to facilitate the attention to detail and quality workmanship necessary for an excellent project.

It is important to maintain a system of checks and balances by using a team that involves a contractor and architect or interior designer who can work together to ensure that all activities are in sync.

About the Author

Gail Green is the founder and principal of Gail Green Interiors, a full-service interior design and decorating firm specializing in upscale residential and commercial projects. Educated at Columbia University and trained at architecture offices, Green has been in the design field for more than 30 years. Her work has been widely published in magazines such as *House Beautiful, House & Garden, Elle Decor, Florida Design, Architectural Digest* and *The New York Times Magazine.*

Green has been a featured designer in the prestigious Kips Bay Decorator Show House and the Southampton, Greenwich, and Southport show houses and has appeared on NBC's *Designer Living,* CNN's *Style with Elsa Klensch,* NBC's *Today* show and in television programming for NYC taxicabs. Green has also designed window displays in New York for the Hermès 57th Street boutique and Baccarat. Her work has appeared in numerous interior design books, and she has lectured widely on related topics, including those of divorce design and small space science.

In addition to being a member of the Women's Forum, the Yale Club of New York City, the Municipal Art Society of New York, the Art Deco Society of New York, the Victorian Society New York and the Institute for Classical Architecture and Art, Green holds advanced degrees in rare books and literature and is a prolific writer on an array of subjects, including art, antiques, food, wine and luxury goods.

About the Architects

David Estreich Architects is a full-service architecture firm based in New York City. Featured in publications such as *Architectural*

Digest, The New York Times, Metropolitan Home and *Florida Design,* David Estreich and Brian Blackburn have become known for their innovative solutions and unique approach to commercial and residential projects.

Acknowledgements
Without the following support, this book would not exist.

*Special thanks to the following photographers
for their wonderful work:*

~ David Estreich ~
~ Phillip Ennis ~
~ Kurt Dolnier ~

*Special thanks to the following architecture firm
for its extraordinary technical insight and expertise:*

~ David Estreich Architects ~

*Special thanks to the following editors and designers
for their exceptional talent, time and dedication:*

~ Jessica Flint ~
~ Rasika Boice ~
~ Elizabeth Schlossberg ~
~ Michele DeFilippo and 1106 Design ~

(Photo illustrations presented throughout include interior design elements by Gail Green Interiors and architecture by David Estreich Architects.)

Sources

The following works detail the fundamental principles, philosophies and concepts expressed within this guide.

Paine, Melanie, *Fabric Magic.* New York: Pantheon Books, 1987.

Lang, Donna, *Decorating with Fabric.* New York: Clarkson Potter, 1986.

Calloway, Stephen. *The Elements of Style.* New York: Simon and Schuster, 1991.

McCloud, Kevin. *Decorative Style.* New York: Simon and Schuster, 1990.

Thornton, Peter. *Authentic Decor: The Domestic Interior 1620–1920.* New York: Viking, 1984

Miller, Judith. *Period Details: A Sourcebook for House Restoration.* New York: Crown, 1987.

Parissien, Steven. *Adam Style.* London: Phaidon, 1992.

Sekler, Eduard. Josef Hoffman. *Salzburg: Residenz Verlag,* 1982.

De Groer, Leon. *Decorative Arts in Europe 1790–1850.* New York: Rizzoli, 1986.

Clifton-Mogg, Caroline. *The Neoclassical Source Book.* New York: Rizzoli, 1991.

Harris, Eileen. *The Genius of Robert Adam.* New Haven: Yale University Press, 2001.

Miller, Judith. *More Period Details.* New York: Clarkson Potter, 1999.

Gravagnuolo, Benedetto. *Adolf Loos.* New York: Rizzoli, 1982.

Bayer, Patricia. *Art Deco Interiors.* London: Thames & Hudson, 1990.

Hageney, Wolfgang. *Repertoire: Modern Interior Design 1928–1929.* Rome: Belvedere, 1986.

White, Samuel G. *The Houses of McKim, Mead & White.* New York: Rizzoli, 1998.

Arwas, Victor. *Art Deco.* New York: Harry Abrams, 1992.

Dufrene, Maurice. *Authentic Art Deco Interiors.* Suffolk: Antique Collectors' Club, 1989.

Goguel, Solange. *Rene Herbst.* Paris, Editions du Regard, 1990.

Brunhammer, Yvonne. *French Decorative Art.* Paris: Flammarion, 1990.

Cliff, Stafford. *The French Archive of Design and Decoration.* New York, Harry N. Abrams, 1999.

Whitton, Sherrill. *Interior Design and Decoration.* New York: J.B. Lippincott, 1974.

Walking, Gillian. *Upholstery Styles.* New York: Van Nostrand Reinhold, 1989.

Gilliatt, Mary. *The Decorating Book.* New York: Pantheon, 1981.

Helsel, Marjorie Borradaile. *The Interior Designer's Drapery Bedspread & Canopy Sketchfile.* New York: Whitney Library of Design, 1990.

Kallir, Jane. *Viennese Design and the Wiener Werkstatte.* New York: Galerie St. Etienne, 1986.

Menten, Theodore. *The Art Deco Style.* New York: Dover, 1972.

Wise, Herbert, H. *Attention to Detail.* New York: Quick Fox, 1979.

Varnedoe, Kirk. *Vienna 1990.* New York, Museum of Modern Art. 1986.

Hillier, Bevis. *Art Deco Style.* London: Phaidon Press, 1997.

Day, Susan. *Art Deco and Modernist Carpets.* London: Thames & Hudson, 2002.

Fulweiler, Megan. *Ultimate Decorating.* Lincolnwood: Publications International, 2003.

Schorske, Carl E. *Fin-De-Siecle Vienna.* New York: Vintage Books, 1981.

Cruickshank, Dan. *Sir Banister Fletcher's A History of Architecture.* London: Architectural Press, 1996.

Bonus

CPSIA information can be obtained
at www.ICGtesting.com
Printed in the USA
LVOW05s1540181115

463166LV00049B/317/P